In *Countdown for Couples*, Dale and Susan Mathis have provided couples with the tools they need to build a strong foundation for a lasting marriage. For any couple planning to get married, this book is a must!

—GARY D. CHAPMAN, PH.D.
Author of *The Five Love Languages* and
The Five Languages of Apology

What a gift to every young couple seriously considering marriage! Dale and Susan Mathis have addressed crucial issues in a positive, personal, and passionate way. Their warm approach creates an atmosphere of exploration and honest discourse for young men and women willing to examine themselves and their relationship. Anyone doing premarital counseling can benefit from this workbook-style resource.

—LOUIS MCBURNEY, M.D.
Marble Retreat Worldwide

So many couples spend months preparing for their wedding day but take almost no time to prepare their hearts and minds for the marriage that will last a lifetime! *Countdown for Couples* is an excellent resource that tackles issues such as expectations, finances, in-law challenges, and more. Take time to read what Dale and Susan Mathis have put together. You'll be so glad you did!

—PETER J. LARSON, PH.D.
Vice President of PREPARE/ENRICH

Countdown for Couples

FOCUS ON THE FAMILY®

Countdown for Couples

PREPARING FOR THE ADVENTURE OF MARRIAGE

Dale Mathis, M.A. & Susan Mathis

Tyndale House Publishers, Inc.
CAROL STREAM, ILLINOIS

A Focus on the Family book published by Tyndale House Publishers Inc., Carol Stream, Illinois 60188

TYNDALE and Tyndale's quill logo are registered trademarks of Tyndale House Publishers Inc.

Focus on the Family and the accompanying logo and design are federally registered trademarks of Focus on the Family, Colorado Springs, CO 80995.

Certain people's names and specific details of their stories have been changed to protect the privacy of the individuals involved.

The use or recommendation of material from various Web sites does not imply endorsement of those sites in their entirety.

Editor: Brandy Bruce
Cover design: Ron Kaufmann
Cover photograph of couple holding hands copyright © by Veer. All rights reserved.
Cover photograph of jewelry box copyright © by Rubberball/Getty Images. All rights reserved.
Cover photograph of flower copyright © by Steven Miric/iStockphoto. All rights reserved.
Cover photograph of calendar copyright © by Gary Woodard/iStockphoto. All rights reserved.
Cover photograph of check copyright © by Sladjana Lukic/iStockphoto. All rights reserved.
Cover and interior pattern copyright © by Christina Rodriguez/iStockphoto. All rights reserved.
Cover photograph of bride copyright © by Gina deConti. All rights reserved.
Authors' photo by Lexie Rhodes.

Library of Congress Cataloging-in-Publication Data
Mathis, Dale, 1941-
  Countdown for couples : preparing for the adventure of marriage / Dale Mathis and Susan Mathis.
    p. cm.
  ISBN-13: 978-1-58997-485-2
  ISBN-10: 1-58997-485-9
  1. Marriage—Religious aspects—Christianity. I. Mathis, Susan, 1957- II. Title.
  BV835.M2765 2007
  248.8'44—dc22

                                2007031880

Printed in the United States of America
4 5 6 7 8 9 / 17 16 15 14

Dedicated to our five adult children:
To Mark, for your creative spirit
To Bruce, for your gift as a physician
To Erik, for your dedication to the education of children
To Sean, for your love of God's creation
To Janelle, for your passion to help the poor
and take the gospel around the world

And to you, our readers, who are preparing for the adventure
of marriage with wisdom and discernment.
To each of you—and to each of your mates—may God's love
live in your hearts and lives.

CONTENTS

Acknowledgments

How can we begin to thank each of you who has influenced us and imparted wisdom through the years so that now we can share God's truth with others?

Thanks to the members of our families, especially Susan's mom and our adult children—you have journeyed through life with us during the good times as well as the tough times. Each of you has enlarged us in incredible ways.

Thanks to our friends who have enriched our lives—and to those who graciously shared your stories with us and with our readers. This book is richer because of you.

Thanks to the team at Focus on the Family who worked so hard to make this project all it can be: Larry, Brandy, Cami, Kellie—and to our friends and colleagues in the periodicals and family ministry departments, especially Pam, Andrea, Sheila, and Scott, who supported us through it all.

Thanks to each of you who has encouraged and helped us see beyond our inabilities so we can tap into His abilities. We trust you realize who you are and how much you mean to us.

Thanks to you, our readers, for entrusting your hearts and your relationships to God's Word and these pages as you get ready for the best adventure in life—marriage.

And most of all, thanks to God. May we ever live to know You and make You known.

GETTING STARTED

Isn't it great? The thought of marrying the one you love, the ecstatic feelings of sheer happiness, the excitement of planning a wedding and counting down the days. But wait! There's all that other stuff—the "for better *or worse*, for richer *or poorer*, *in sickness* and in health, till *death* do us part"—the daily living-together stuff.

Marriage is a huge commitment and not to be taken lightly, so you're wise to take the time to assess your relationship and learn all you can before your big day. This book will help you do just that. We'll review the basics, such as what love is really all about, but we'll also go deeper and address things you may never have thought you needed—or wanted—to talk about.

If you see this premarital preparation as a countdown to an adventure, a journey that will take you deeper into the life of the one you love, it'll be one of the most exciting and important things you've done together so far. That's the way we viewed our premarital learning, and even today we see it as one of the greatest gifts we have given each other.

This book provides premarital information based on a biblical worldview that is practical, time-tested, sound, insightful, and most of all, useful. By sharing the truth of God's Word on the subject of marriage preparation, we hope to help you better understand God's plan for this awesome aspect of life.

Here are the four main purposes of this book:

- To help you better understand yourself, your future spouse, and your future together
- To alleviate your fears, doubts, and worries about yourself, your future mate, and your marriage
- To prepare you for living together and loving each other forever
- To launch you on your marriage journey and a lifetime of growing together

As you use this book to prepare for your marriage, you'll explore many facets of who you are, who the one you love is, and what it will be like to live together and love each other for the rest of your lives. You'll talk about the spiritual, emotional, social, relational, and physical intricacies of being married.

You'll also review your past and understand better how your family and your experiences have molded your life. You'll try to articulate your expectations, beliefs, attitudes, concerns, fears, and struggles about marriage, and even assess how ready you are to marry at this time. And you'll grow to know your future mate better—more than you ever dreamed possible.

You'll hear from experts on such topics as communication, marital roles, in-law challenges, sexuality, finances, conflict resolution, and so on. The following chapters will also provide you with extensive resources for continuing to grow in your marriage throughout your entire life together.

A couple who is willing to take the time to prepare for marriage and sees the value in doing the work it takes to get ready will often have the same attitude and behavior after marriage. And the opposite is true too. If one of you thinks you know it all, beware! That same resistance to work on your relationship may hinder your marriage from growing to its full potential.

Be careful that you don't enter marriage hoping to change your future mate, or you'll likely be disappointed. Lifetime habits don't usually change; people are who they are. Walk into this preparation time with the view that you want to know yourself and your future mate better. Be willing to grow together, learning new ways to make your marriage a success. Hey, you're mature enough to realize that neither of you is perfect!

To be effective, it's essential that you choose, right now, to be open, honest, and vulnerable with each other. If you try to hide anything, we can almost guarantee that it'll come up after you marry, and by that time, it might be much more hurtful to your spouse and your relationship than it will be now. By talking through the issues before you marry, you'll build trust, understanding, and intimacy.

As you work through the pages of this book, we suggest you do it with a pastor, a counselor, a mature couple, or a small group. Other people can help you through areas that are confusing, scary, or hard to discuss. They can provide you with a fresh perspective when you need it and keep you accountable.

But if you choose to go through the book without outside help, both of you need to commit to working through every chapter. Set aside a specific time each week to read through one chapter, or maybe two, and allot time for discussion.

Part of our motivation for writing this book is to help you explore areas we were too unaware of, too naive, or too inexperienced to know how to handle in our first marriages. Since we both experienced the trauma, grief, and heartache of failed marriages early in our adulthood, we want to prevent others—especially you—from going through the same experience.

We're also aware that one of the reasons for our failures is that we didn't have a manual like this to help us ask the tough questions before we said "I do." Marriage can get complicated, and knowing some of its complexities and secrets ahead of time can help you be more successful than you could ever be without preparation. We hope to help you avoid frustrations, hurts, and failures by informing you about those issues that can cause trouble for couples.

In fact, I [Dale] decided to get my first master's degree in counseling in 1971 so I could identify some of what went wrong with my first marriage, learn how not to make the same mistakes, and help others avoid them too.

Though I earned my advanced degrees in secular universities, I'm convinced that Christ at the center of a marriage makes all the difference.

I [Susan] have been honored to choose, review, edit, and publish literally thousands of articles on marriage and family life during my tenure as *Focus on the Family* magazine editor and editorial director, and I've learned truths that have helped me and countless others.

As we wrote this book, we not only had lots of fun together, but we also learned so much from and about each other, all of which helps us in helping others. As a couple, we consider it a privilege and a joy to regularly empower future mates to start out on the right path together, whether we're working as facilitators in our church's premarital ministry, with a young couple still in college, or in private counseling with an older couple. In our years of serving in premarital ministry, we've found that couples who take the time to really prepare for their future together walk into marriage with a confidence and security they wouldn't have otherwise.

Throughout the book, you'll read about some of the lessons we learned the hard way. We'll also share stories of other couples and their successes and struggles. We know you'll make your own mistakes along the way, but we assure you that the Lord will faithfully walk you through them as you trust in Him. Our prayer is that you'll make fewer and far less serious mistakes than we made in our first marriages.

We suggest you work through this book at your own pace, but try not to skip too quickly through topics you think you understand. We also recommend that you do no more than two chapters per week. You may find you need to slow down when you hit speed bumps where the two of you disagree, or when you find it difficult to work through a topic.

But don't give up. Persevere together. Take your time and glean everything you can from each chapter. Whether this is your first marriage or, like us, you've experienced a failed marriage and are hoping to avoid making the same mistakes again, this book offers the practical advice and tools you need to succeed. And if you find you need more help with a specific topic, you can read the sidebars throughout the book, where experts discuss the topic. Get their books, check out their Web sites, and find out more.

In addition to your reading this book, Susan and I [Dale] strongly encourage you to assess your relationship by taking the Premarital Personal and Relationship Inventory (PREPARE), an assessment used by professional counselors, pastors, trained and certified mentors, and churches that conduct premarital courses. (For more information, go to www.family.org/couple checkup.) We've used this assessment with numerous couples and find it to be accurate and reliable.

By taking the PREPARE, you can assess your potential for marital success as well as learn about the strengths and weaknesses in your relationship. Then you can discuss issues, some which are difficult or may have been overlooked. The objective is to encourage and inform, not to discourage you.

By reading this book and taking the PREPARE, you'll begin marriage with some newly acquired skills. You'll also gain an understanding and appreciation of your future mate as well as get to know yourself better. Your expectations will be more realistic, and you'll be more committed to your marriage.

Finally, please know that we've changed many of the names in our stories to protect the individuals' privacy, but the examples are real-life situations couples face.

Now, let's get started.

1

A MARRIAGE OF THREE

What's God's View of Love and Marriage?

I [Susan] was so excited. Dale and I had driven to Estes Park, Colorado, to get away and visit some friends. We sat gazing at the beautiful mountains, asking question after question of each other and discussing the possibility of our future together. Before considering marriage, we had promised to reveal our thoughts, fears, goals, and needs to each other completely.

After our time in the mountains, every night for several weeks Dale and I went through lists we'd made of things we wanted to know about each other—everything from how we were raised to finances to roles and goals to expectations and pet peeves to sex and health issues to our relationships with God, and so much more.

As adults, we had both been single for more than a decade. We'd been deeply hurt by our earlier failed relationships, and we worried that we might not be able to be successful in the future. Although we had tried to learn all we could about love, relationships, and God's plan for marriage, being open and honest with each other made us feel very vulnerable. We realized that this kind of openness could make or break our budding relationship. But we also decided that without complete honesty, we'd both be marrying a person we didn't really know.

We realized that we needed to start by establishing a solid foundation for our relationship.

Scripture says, "Where there is no vision, the people perish" (Proverbs 29:18, KJV). In addition to talking through important topics and sharing our feelings with each other, we discovered a principle we want to share with you: The best way to begin planning for your future together is by deciding now what your vision is for your marriage.

What did this look like for us? Dale and I agreed that our vision was to live the message of Jesus Christ's redeeming love through our relationship. By caring for each other physically, emotionally, spiritually, and every other way, we wanted to create a fully intimate and inspiring relationship that could show our children and grandchildren, family, and friends the beauty and promise of God's plan for marriage.

Every couple's vision will be different, of course, but a clear vision for your marriage will guide, inspire, and motivate you as you grow through the stresses of life. When you have a positive and exciting vision for life together, you can work toward that goal, even when times are tough.

A vision for your marriage goes far beyond just learning and practicing relationship skills. Understanding God's perspective is critical to the success of your marriage.

God has given us that vision in His Word. He has given us His definition of love, His blueprint for covenant commitment, and His grace-filled plan for marriage.

Let's take a closer look at God's design for marriage.

THE VERY FIRST MARRIAGE

When God created the first marriage between Adam and Eve, He said it wasn't good for man to be alone (Genesis 2:18). Why? Because we're all made in His image, the image of a completely relational God—Father, Son, and Holy Spirit who work together unselfishly for the good of humankind and

Ask the Expert

Author Al Janssen imagines the moment of creation and a heavenly scene in his book *Your Marriage Masterpiece*:

"Amazing." Abdiel watched as God stepped back, glowing with pride, and the man and woman gazed at each other, touching only their fingertips. "Yes, God has created two like Himself . . ."

"Not exactly like Him," corrected Zephon.

"No, not the same. Yet, you see glimpses of Him in the two of them together."

Zephon understood. "Yes, He is three yet one. They are two yet one."

"Two, maybe. But with the Creator that makes three!"

By now, all of the angelic audience saw what Abdiel and Zephon had recognized. In this man and woman, joined together, God had provided a reflection of Himself for all His creation. Two incredible creatures, brilliant and beautiful, each unique, but together revealing deeper aspects of the intricate beauty of their Creator.

Truly, this was a work of art. This was God's masterpiece.[1]

In *Your Marriage Masterpiece*, Janssen shows us how God's vision for marriage is His supreme artistic achievement. He teaches us how we can make our marriages fulfilling and reflect God's masterpiece in our relationships with our future mates.

for God's purposes. Because we were created to be like Him, there's an inner yearning for that same deep, intimate relationship.

Adam and Eve exemplified the deepest, most intimate relationship as a couple. Scripture says they were naked and not ashamed (Genesis 2:25), not just in a physical, sexual way, but, we think, they were "naked" emotionally, spiritually, and intellectually as well. They were vulnerable with each other. From the very first married couple, we see that marriage is taking two unique people and uniting their souls and bodies for a common purpose, for the rest of their lives.

What Is Marriage?

Marriage is the legal, social, and spiritual contract between a man and a woman. It's a covenant agreement made before God. It's a commitment to each other—a pledge to live together, to serve each other, and to remain faithful to one another. Marriage is also God's way of showing His love for us, showing His marriage plan to the world, and helping us become more like Him.

Socially, marriage is a public contract that says "We are one" as we share our lives with others. Emotionally, it's being vulnerable, transparent, and honest with each other as with no one else. Intellectually, it's sharing our thoughts, opinions, and desires with each other. Physically, it's everything from a tender kiss to passionate sexual intercourse. Spiritually, it's praying together, worshiping together, and growing together in our faith.

Marriage is about working on our character; extending love, grace, and forgiveness to each other; and growing through our mistakes. None of us is perfect, and understanding and accepting this up front is important. We are all works in progress. When we see marriages fail, we sometimes think those marriages must have been mistakes. But remember, marriage is taking two imperfect people and putting them in a committed relationship so they can safely grow and mature together as they work on their imperfections and problems. It's about giving, helping, trusting, forgiving, caring, learning, and living through the ups and downs of life.

What Is Love?

If marriage is a picture of God's love for us as well as an opportunity to show love to each other, it's imperative that we have a good understanding of what love is. But how can we define *love*?

A good place to start is the Bible. The Love Chapter is 1 Corinthians 13. You've probably heard it before. But what does it really say? Let's look at verses 4–8.

> Love is patient, love is kind. It does not envy, it does not boast, it is not proud. It is not rude, it is not self-seeking, it is not easily angered, it keeps no record of wrongs. Love does not delight in evil but rejoices with the truth. It always protects, always trusts, always hopes, always perseveres.
>
> Love never fails.

Most, if not all, of us have tasted the pain of love lost, and none of us wants to experience that again. These few verses provide a good framework to help us understand how we can love well. They show us the ideal, the perfect model of love. But the truth is that although the characteristics of love are great, we don't always love perfectly. Sometimes we simply fall short. If you understand this, you'll give each other space and grace to make mistakes. And God can use your marriage to show others that real love and grace can make people different, even better.

Throughout this book we'll continue to unpack 1 Corinthians 13 as you learn how to better love the way God intended for you to love each other. You'll also learn practical and helpful ways to put God's love into practice.

WHAT'S COVENANT COMMITMENT?

In our living room there is a symbol we used in our wedding ceremony. It's a three-strand cord of red, white, and gold. For us, it symbolizes that the commitment we made to marriage wasn't just between the two of us. The covenant was made by three of us, with God at the center. Scripture says, "A cord of three strands is not quickly broken" (Ecclesiastes 4:12).

A commitment to marry is more than just signing a contract. Marriage is a sacred covenant, a plan God created for our benefit. In the Bible we read that God made covenants with His people. But people like Jonathan and David, Ruth and Naomi, and others also made covenants *with each other*. They were committing to love, serve, and care for each other. Covenant promises are unconditional; there are no escape clauses and/or money-back guarantees. Covenants are made on the foundations of faith and love, and they are permanent.

We all know couples, maybe even our own parents, who divorced. Maybe they just grew tired of each other. Or maybe the marriage was plagued by abuse, addiction, or infidelity. Whatever the reason, the couple broke the commitment they made to each other, and the painful consequences of their choice affected many others besides themselves.

But most of us also know couples who have been married for decades and are happy despite the challenges they've faced through the years. Our friends Bob and Gayle just celebrated 55 years together. They love each other dearly, are the closest of companions, and remain deeply committed to each other. As Dale says, "When we grow up, let's be just like them!" These are the kinds of couples who can give us hope for our marriages.

As you begin your marriage, it's a good idea to find one or two couples you can look to as a model of what you hope your marriage will eventually look like. Especially if healthy marriages have been rare in your life, looking to others who have successful marriages can be beneficial. We'll talk more about this a little later.

Marriage is all about choice. It's about making the right choices to love, honor, and care for the one you commit your life to, even when it's tough. We have to choose to love each other on a moment-by-moment basis every day of our lives together. This type of commitment involves more than just romantic feelings; it's a choice to be physically, emotionally, mentally, and spiritually faithful to each other every day.

Leaving and Cleaving

Jesus said,

> Haven't you read . . . that at the beginning the Creator made them male and female, and said, "For this reason a man will leave his father and mother and be united to his wife, and the two will become one flesh"? So they are no longer two, but one. Therefore what God has joined together, let man not separate. (Matthew 19:4–6)

Leaving and cleaving—uniting—are choices every married person must make to leave his or her parents and the single lifestyle and to cleave to the union, security, intimacy, joy, and even struggles of life with his or her spouse.

When a couple enjoys this covenant commitment, when they truly leave and cleave, they feel secure emotionally and physically. A wife feels that her husband is truly devoted to her and looking out for her best interests. A husband has the surety that he is important, valued, a priority, and worthy of investment or sacrifice. This is why cohabitation before marriage lacks permanence and creates a false sense of security. A relationship without covenant commitment lacks true intimacy.

Karen misunderstood the concept of leaving and cleaving early in her marriage with Rick. As soon as they returned from their honeymoon, she started calling her mother daily. She shared with her mother the most intimate details of her marriage, and she relied on her mother's advice and opinions for everything. Soon Rick began to feel betrayed, so he quietly stepped into the background and busied himself with other activities until he couldn't take it anymore.

It took several painful discussions before Karen understood that she needed to leave and cleave to Rick. Of course she needed her mother, but she also needed to leave the single life and family ties of her childhood. When she married, she became "one" with her husband, and she needed to act accordingly. That meant putting him first when it came to her time, interests, privacy, and more.

This covenant you're about to make affects more than the two of you. It affects everyone who comes to your wedding, everyone you know. When you say your vows before an audience on your wedding day, you'll be doing much more than performing a ceremony and allowing your friends and family to celebrate a special occasion with you. They are witnesses to a sacred covenant, which you freely choose to enter into. But while we want to emphasize the fact that marriage is a major commitment and takes work, we also want to assure you that the right kind of marriage can be the greatest blessing of your lives.

Congratulations! You're on your way to becoming ready for the most amazing adventure of life: marriage!

What About Me?

Looking back on what you've learned about covenant and commitment, each of you write your own definition of a covenant commitment in marriage.

What About Us?

What's your vision for marriage? Read Psalm 127:1, Proverbs 24:3–4, and Matthew 7:24–27.

Having a marital vision is having common goals that are bigger than your everyday circumstances and feelings. Maybe you hope to be a couple who strives to support and build up each other, helping one another reach your full potential. Maybe you have a deep desire for your marriage to be a place of safety and love. Maybe you want your marriage to be an adventure in which you work together to make your goals and dreams come true.

Whatever your vision is, make a united plan and be strategic about carrying it out. Set goals for your marriage.

List five things you want to include in the vision for your marriage.

1.

2.

3.

4.

5.

Share with each other what your vision for your marriage entails. What does it look like to you? How will you fulfill it? Your ideas may be different, but that's okay.

If your ideas are different, you'll need to work together to find a united vision in the midst of those differences. If you can't resolve your differences, be sure to consult with someone who can help you work through them now. As you develop and refine a clear vision for your marriage, the exciting vision of the marriage God has for you will become clear to you. Revisit your vision statement often. Establish one-, two-, and five-year goals as well as a lifetime vision.

Just for Fun!

What one question would you like to ask God?

What event in the Bible would you most have liked to witness?

What Does God Say?

Read the following scriptures together, and answer three or more of the questions as you reflect on what you've read so far.

> For this reason a man will leave his father and mother and be united to his wife, and the two will become one flesh. (Ephesians 5:31)

How do a man and a woman become one?

> Jesus replied: " 'Love the Lord your God with all your heart and with all your soul and with all your mind.' This is the first and greatest commandment. And the second is like it: 'Love your neighbor as yourself.' " (Matthew 22:37–39)

What are God's priorities for love?

> You, my brothers, were called to be free. But do not use your freedom to indulge the sinful nature; rather, serve one another in love. (Galatians 5:13)

How should you love each other?

> A new command I give you: Love one another. As I have loved you,
> so you must love one another. By this all men will know that you are
> my disciples, if you love one another. (John 13:34–35)

As a couple, what's your ultimate purpose on earth?

Read Ephesians 5:22–33 in your Bible. What is God's vision for your marriage?

2

READY OR NOT

Are You Ready for a Lifelong Commitment?

Shortly after Susan and I [Dale] were engaged, I was diagnosed with prostate cancer. I was shocked because I'd been so healthy all my life. The word *cancer* is extra frightening to me since my older brother died of kidney cancer at the age of 17.

The conflicting emotions made my heart pound—the fear of dying much sooner than expected and the thoughts of having to choose a treatment, as well as undergoing possible side effects. Then I thought about Susan. How would I tell her, and how would she react? What if the cancer spread, and our journey together ended earlier than we had anticipated? How could this happen now, just when we were planning our future together? I knew I was about to face the toughest battle of my life.

First, I had to tell Susan and give her the opportunity to back out of our engagement. I knew this promise we were about to make—to love and serve each other through sickness and health—shouldn't have to be tested until long after we were married. At least, that's what I thought.

I told her everything. I explained to her the treatment options—

none of which were appealing—and then I had to tell her that after treatment, there was more than a 50 percent chance of impotency. I'm sure she was terrified, but she had already made the decision to marry me, even if cancer took one of us sooner than we would ever have dreamed.

We cried and we prayed for courage and wisdom to make the right choices, for healing, and for a long life together. We did our homework, got four doctors' opinions, and proceeded with the treatment. Our first year of marriage was filled with a multitude of challenges, concerns, fears, and worries.

What got us through this difficult time was believing that God had a plan for our lives together. As it turned out, this book was inspired by the knowledge that we're here for such a brief time and that God wants us to make a difference in other people's lives while we can. We smile about it now, especially when one of our friends quipped that Susan should have had me inspected before we got engaged. Yet today we're thankful that the cancer is in remission, and our marriage is stronger because of this trial. Through the pain and fear of that first year together, we learned firsthand the meaning of lifelong commitment and sacrifice.

As we counsel couples, we often ask why they want to marry each other. They typically answer, "Because we love each other!" While that's great and expected, there are often many underlying reasons for wanting to marry that may require some deeper soul searching. Understanding those reasons may help you assess whether you're ready to make a lifelong commitment.

Do you know why you want to be married? Could it be because all your friends are getting married? Do you feel eager to leave your parents' home? Is your biological clock ticking? Maybe you're rebounding from a broken relationship or a divorce. Maybe you're marrying because of an unexpected pregnancy. Or perhaps you think marriage will end your loneliness. You may think marriage will make you feel whole and make your life more meaningful. Maybe you feel guilty about having premarital sex and think that marriage will relieve your guilt.

You might feel that getting married is the expected thing to do when you reach a certain age. Your peers, your parents, or maybe even the culture you live in may have influenced you to feel that way.

Whatever your answer, you should understand the real reasons you want to marry. All too often people make this important decision prematurely or without enough knowledge of what's driving them toward this goal. They count down the days till their wedding with little thought of the lifetime commitment that begins that day.

It's wise to take time to review the reasons many couples give for wanting to be married and see if any of them describe you. Maybe several of these reasons apply to you; just be honest with yourself. The more specific you are in answering this question, the deeper and better you'll understand yourself.

Ask the Experts

In Dr. James and Shirley Dobson's book *Night Light: A Devotional for Couples*, the authors share daily devotional stories, which offer encouragement, practical advice, and biblical truths, for couples to read through together. They share the following:

> There is nothing quite like being loved unconditionally and intimately, decade after decade, by someone who promises to be there for better or worse, in sickness and health, whether richer or poorer, forsaking all others—*all* others—until separated by death. It is a plan that bears the wisdom and compassion of the Creator Himself.[1]

You may have other reasons we haven't mentioned, and that's okay too. Understand that we're not saying your reason for marrying is wrong, but it does help to know what's motivating you. The idea is to have a reality check and explore your innermost desires and needs. You'll grow in the process.

After you've assessed your own motives, it's just as important to try to determine why your partner may want to marry you. This may prove to be more difficult, but it's just as necessary. The purpose of this assessment isn't to convince you to break off your relationship; it's meant to help you gain a better understanding of who you're choosing to spend the rest of your life with and why.

This chapter is designed to sort out these age-old questions and to help you make sure you know yourself and your future mate before you marry him or her. Hopefully, it will be revealing and awaken your heart to understanding yourself and your loved one better.

Take a few minutes to finish the following statements. Take turns and answer as honestly as possible.

1. I love you because . . . (Name at least three reasons why you love this person.)
2. I want to marry you because . . . (Name three or more reasons for marrying this person. Be as specific as you can. "I love you" is too general.)
3. We're a good match because . . . (Name up to five reasons that explain why you think you're compatible.)

WARNING: DANGER AHEAD!

Evaluating your motives for getting married is only one aspect of determining whether you're truly ready to make a lifelong commitment to your future mate. The truth is that sometimes we love a person who is missing the mark big time. This section will give you an opportunity to take a good look at your relationship. The red flags we'll discuss aren't meant to frighten you or to cause friction in your relationship. But these important topics must be addressed before you make a lifelong commitment to each other.

Anne lived many years in an unhealthy marriage because she didn't heed the warning signs. She knew that Kevin cheated on his tests in college and "fibbed" a bit, but she believed that he would change as he matured, as many people do. She refused to see his regular self-centeredness and dishonesty as warning signs. She overlooked the fact that she often couldn't trust what he was saying. She didn't believe his excuses, and his stories didn't match up with reality. She thought that loving Kevin meant she could never question him and that she had to forgive everything and press on. But despite her efforts, their marriage ended when Kevin went to live with another woman.

Anne didn't understand that being patient, forgiving, and trusting toward the one you love doesn't mean turning a blind eye to unhealthy behaviors, and it doesn't mean putting up with immature, out-of-control, or angry behavior, especially if it's a regular pattern. Most of us feel uncomfortable, unsure, or guilty about our thoughts, feelings, and behaviors when something's wrong. If you're experiencing these types of feelings about yourself, your partner, or your future marriage, now is the time to delve deeper into why you're feeling this way.

If your future spouse isn't trustworthy and faithful, you're asking for trouble. Little white lies, withholding information, and keeping secrets are BIG red flags, signs that must not be overlooked. You may not have even realized it until now, but if your future mate shows signs of dishonesty, or if you can't trust what he or she says or does, beware!

Because we're imperfect people, we're all a bit selfish sometimes. We're often moody or insecure, and we sometimes get angry or become a little inconsiderate of others. But these behaviors should be the exception, not the norm. What you're trying to assess is whether your future mate has a pattern of negative, selfish, or self-centered behavior, which will hurt you and your marriage.

Because you're deep into this relationship already, it may be difficult to make these kinds of assessments. But it's very possible that the negative patterns you've seen in your loved one's behavior won't change, and you'll likely be living with those behaviors for the rest of your life.

I [Susan] knew that if I ever fell for someone, I would likely lose my perspective and discernment, so I had Dale "interrogated" by several of my friends—okay, 34 of my friends! Their insight was so wise, helping me to not only see why I was so interested in this man but to also feel free to set aside my fears and concerns about making a lifetime commitment to Dale.

In fact, one of my most respected friends made sure he and his wife knew where they stood in their opinion of the man I would one day marry. Dale was at the point where he knew we were meant for each other, but I was still a little scared. So I thought I'd have "Uncle Phil" slow things down by having him and his wife, Joyce, over for an "interrogation dinner."

After answering some tough and challenging questions, Dale apparently passed the test. Phil leaned over to me and said, "So why don't you marry him already?" Joyce playfully swatted Phil's arm, and I swatted the other, but he was right. Dale and I were ready to be married, even though Dale and I opted against Phil's offer to loan us Joyce's wedding ring and marry us right then and there!

RECOGNIZING THE RED FLAGS

After years of counseling and mentoring couples of all ages and backgrounds, we've identified a number of red flags that should alert you to possible trouble spots in a relationship. If any of these danger signs show up, be sure to slow down and reevaluate your relationship, taking the time to see if there is a possible resolution before you move ahead. You might talk with a pastor, counselor, or trusted mentor regarding your concerns.

Read through the following list of red flags. Some topics may require more discussion than others.

1. Sex before marriage. The truth is that once a couple becomes sexually active, the relationship takes on radically different dynamics. Your perceptions of each other can become distorted, making it more difficult for real intimacy to develop. You may find that you have different priorities and motivations. Your perspective of your future mate may change as well, and you may struggle with long-term trust issues. You may think you know him or her on a genuine, deep, and personal level because you've shared your bodies, but do you really?

The problem is that after a couple becomes sexually involved, they may feel committed to marry despite the fact that they may not know each other well, they may have doubts about their relationship, or family and friends may disapprove. A sense of indebtedness or guilt often sets in, and it's nearly impossible to make a wise decision, especially one as important as a lifelong commitment. For a marriage to be successful, both partners must show evidence of maturity and responsibility; sexual involvement isn't enough.

Although plenty of people have deep regrets about their sexual activity outside of marriage (you might be one of them), you'll rarely find a couple who regrets having saved themselves sexually for marriage. Let us state up front that regardless of whether you've made big mistakes in this area or small ones, God can redeem any situation. We simply want you to talk openly together about this issue. Be honest about your past sexual experiences (though it may not be necessary to share all the details). And take heart that if you've failed in this area, all is not lost. Ask God for forgiveness, ask forgiveness of each other, and choose to remain chaste until your wedding night.

2. Not knowing each other well. Have you had enough time to really get to know each other? Many people don't really know what they're looking for in the first place. Relationships based on such clichés as finding one's "knight in shining armor" or marrying "a raving beauty" will rarely last the test of time.

Do you know exactly what you're looking for in a mate? When you know what you're looking for, you can assess whether your future mate fits that bill. Knowing each other on a real and honest level will reveal to you whether you're compatible.

Jenny met Chris at a church function, and the two struck up a conver-

Remarriage and Blended Families

Some of you may be remarrying and/or possibly creating a blended family. Because there are more people, is more history, and often are more hurts in remarriages and blended-family marriages, these relationships have unique needs that first marriages don't. There are exes and former in-laws who will always be a part of your lives if you have children, as well as other relationships connected to previous marriages. Financial challenges are often carried over from a previous marriage, scheduling situations may be more complex if you have children, and there may be numerous logistical intricacies. And then there's the inevitable emotional baggage that can often affect your new relationship.

So how can you prepare to navigate through these challenges? First, be realistic and proactive in preparing for remarriage. You know there will be tough times. You know it'll be more complicated. So prepare for it. We recommend you use the principles throughout these chapters, such as analyzing your motivations, getting to know each other better, learning to prioritize, and discovering God's plan for your marriage. And for many remarriages, professional counseling is also important.

Take your time and go through the following questions. If you have trouble answering a question, meet with a counselor or a pastor for a different perspective and some extra help.

sation. She was amazed at how much they had in common. They could talk endlessly, never tiring of each other. After just two months of dating, both felt convinced that they belonged together. They had a whirlwind wedding, eagerly jumping headfirst into married life.

(continued)

- Have you recovered from the loss of your previous marriage?
- Have your kids recovered?
- Has your fiancé(e) recovered from the loss of his or her previous marriage?
- Have his or her kids recovered?
- How will this marriage be different from your previous marriage?
- What are your unique needs as a remarried couple and/or a blended family?
- What do you expect from this marriage and/or your blended family?
- How will you manage your finances, especially when it comes to child support?
- If you've been on your own for a long time, how will you become interdependent in this new marriage?
- Are you comfortable with your ex and/or the relationship your fiancé(e) has with his or her ex? Do either of you anticipate potential problems in this area? If so, explain.
- Are you prepared for the complexities of being a stepparent?
- Are there child-custody issues, legal matters, or other concerns that may cause problems in the future? If so, take some time to talk through those concerns.
- What will be required for you to have a successful journey as a remarried couple and create a healthy blended-family life?

But within weeks Jenny discovered that Chris was an avid video gamer. She couldn't believe how much time and money he was willing to invest in games. Chris soon realized that Jenny enjoyed entertaining. His introverted nature clashed with her desire to invite friends over every weekend. It didn't take long for annoying habits and different personalities and interests to drive the two apart. More than once Jenny asked herself what she'd seen in Chris at the beginning. And Chris wondered why he had once thought they had so much in common.

If you haven't given your relationship time to unfold, take some time now to make an objective list of qualities you hope to find in a potential mate. (Your list should reflect the qualities you'd want in any future mate, not just the qualities you see in your present relationship.) Then make sure your future mate fits your list well. You'll be glad you took time to do this.

3. *Bad habits.* Habits diametrically opposed to your tastes, values, and desires may be as simple as whether your future mate smokes or chews tobacco, or whether he or she has bad table manners or poor hygiene, chews gum incessantly, or is sloppy or lazy. You may be able to ignore these habits now, but they will likely become a problem later. Can you live with a man who only showers twice a week? Can you live with a woman who cracks her gum every minute of the day? Anything from pet peeves to serious personality problems need to be addressed. We'll tackle some of these issues further in the "What About Me?" section at the end of the chapter.

4. *Immaturity.* Melissa couldn't believe it. On her birthday, no less, Barry left her to run an errand for his mother. Whenever Barry's mom or dad called him, Barry jumped and did whatever he was told. Would he continue this pattern if Melissa were to marry him? She suspected so and backed out of that relationship before she was sorry.

Are both of you emotionally mature enough for marriage? Is your future mate still dependent on Mom and Dad for emotional or financial support . . . or are you? Does your future mate take responsibility for his or her own relationship with God? Do both of you have strong decision-making skills?

Are you happy with your present careers? Where do you fit on your future mate's list of priorities?

It's true that most people mature as they grow older, but now is the time to lay the groundwork for your future life together. Remembering to speak the truth in love, voice any concerns either of you has regarding your answers to the previous questions.

5. A critical nature. Is your partner critical of you or of people in general? Joe felt that Jessica was often critical of his appearance, his social skills, and his job status. Because he loved her, he tried to overlook her critical attitude. Yet after they married, Jessica's continued criticisms made Joe feel that he could do nothing right. So he withdrew from her, spending more hours at work. He found fulfillment by becoming a successful businessman, but he and Jessica grew further apart.

Being overly critical can be a sign of a person's own insecurities. Take a moment and evaluate whether you and/or your future mate have been overly critical of each other. Constructive or gentle correction can be a positive action, but marrying someone who is more likely to criticize you than build you up is asking for a life filled with hurt, frustration, and confrontation.

6. Financial irresponsibility. Our culture and the media bombard us with advertisements inviting us to constantly spend money, whether we have it or not. We have credit-card balances we can't repay and loans we can't afford, but we seem to want more than we really need.

After they accumulated more than forty thousand dollars in debt, Mike and Cheri's marriage was on the brink of disaster. Another loan wasn't going to solve things. They needed to get control of their spending and change their lifestyles if their marriage was going to survive. Harsh disagreements and constantly blaming each other only added to the tension and frustration at home. The couple finally downsized and learned to live on a budget, but the cost to the closeness in their relationship was very high.

Financial mismanagement is easy to spot early in a relationship. If your future mate is constantly trying to impress you by spending more than he has, or if she's buying the latest fashions even though she can't afford them, he or she may be financially irresponsible or immature. Recognizing these signs now can save you from heartache later. We'll talk more about this important subject in chapter 8.

7. Abuse. Is there verbal, sexual, physical, emotional, or spiritual abuse in either of your backgrounds? You need to discuss this in depth, and if needed, seek professional counsel to make sure these issues are thoroughly resolved before you marry.

Vick knew Sarah had been physically, sexually, and emotionally abused growing up, but he wanted to rescue her and make her life better. Instead of helping her get healthy, he ignored the warning signs of her chronic anger and insecurities and married her anyway. Just months after they married, Sarah began to abuse Vick with verbal threats, false accusations, and even physical abuse. Now divorced, Sarah continues her unhealthy lifestyle.

If not dealt with adequately, the effects of abuse may hurt your relationship later. Be honest with each other about abuse in your past, and decide together to take the initiative toward healing. Talking with a counselor and joining a support group are two good ways to begin.

In this same way, unhealthy behaviors, such as out-of-control anger, physical abuse, lying, and so on, must be dealt with before moving forward with your relationship. If your partner displays some of these behaviors, be sure to consult a counselor right away.

8. Incompatible belief systems. Regardless of what your chosen faith is, marrying someone who doesn't share your beliefs can be difficult. The Bible tells us not to be "unequally yoked," and for good reason (2 Corinthians 6:14, KJV). Having major faith differences isn't a small matter, especially if you have children.

Kristen came from a Christian background and held to those beliefs, but Eddie didn't share her values or beliefs. Kristen thought for sure that she'd "win" him to Christ with her love, so when Eddie proposed, Kristen happily accepted. But as the years passed, Eddie still refused to share her beliefs. In time Kristen realized that she couldn't force Eddie to participate at church, to engage with her in spiritual discussions, or to pray with her.

Eventually Kristen found it too difficult to juggle her church life with her husband's refusal to live a life of faith, so she simply stopped going to church. When they started a family, Kristen tried to teach their children about prayer and the Bible, but her life no longer matched those values. What at one time seemed like a small issue of differing opinions became a major source of hurt and disappointment in Kristen and Eddie's marriage.

9. Addictions. One of the biggest red flags is when one or both partners in a relationship are addicted to drugs, alcohol, pornography, or gambling, just to name a few. If you and/or your future mate have one or more addictions, you will most likely need professional help to resolve the issue before you marry. Stop and take the necessary time to deal with any addictions before entering a lifelong commitment. Don't deny that an addiction will become a problem for your marriage. It will! We recommend that you talk with a counselor rather than trying to resolve the problem yourself.

10. Selfishness. If your future mate is overly self-centered, selfish, or inconsiderate of you and others, or if he or she always wants things his or her way, watch out! You may be in over your head.

A control freak—that's what you'd call Steve. This macho man saw his wife, Amy, as his servant. Every morning he wanted his coffee prepared for him. Every night he wanted his dinner as soon as he got home from work, and then he expected to enjoy a night of watching sports while Amy caught up on the housework. Amy wanted to be a good wife, but Steve's increasing demands and unkind manners became unbearable. One servant in the family was one too few. Something needed to change.

When Steve's brother Jeff came to visit, he confronted Steve with how he was treating Amy. Fortunately, Steve listened to his big brother and learned to treat Amy with more respect and care.

It takes two people serving each other to make a marriage healthy. This is often overlooked during the dating period because we're usually so enthralled with our own warm, fuzzy feelings of love that we tend to forget to look beyond outward appearances and get to know what our future mate is really like below the surface. When we're dating, we often put our best foot forward, masking our inner selves. But it's critical to look past the outward show to know each other and to learn to serve each other. Does your future mate treat you with respect? Does he or she make your feelings and needs a priority?

At the beginning of this chapter, I [Dale] mentioned my battle with cancer. Susan and I had been married for only four months when I went through cancer surgery. After another four months, I had to have rotator-cuff surgery. Susan stood by me through it all, sacrificing her time, energy, and emotional strength to care for me. I did the same for her when she faced her own battle with cancer.

These experiences taught us that serving each other in healthy ways (showing respect, care, and sacrifice) can make a marriage strong, but selfishness in a marriage will destroy the relationship.

A perfect score of zero in all of the previous categories is highly unlikely, but pay close attention to obvious danger signs. All too often, people marry before they have enough information about each other, and divorce is frequently the result. Dating is such a fun experience that we often get caught up in the thrill of it all, and we unintentionally forget to look deeper. Despite the fact that we know no one is flawless, we fool ourselves into thinking we've found the perfect partner. But the truth is, we all have bad habits and weaknesses, so we have to be realistic about ourselves and our future mates.

What About Me?

Describe the five most important qualities you expect in a marriage relationship.

What characteristics or behaviors would you find absolutely intolerable in a future spouse? (Be specific about pet peeves or annoying habits.)

What pet peeves or habits of yours might frustrate or irritate your future mate? Are you willing to make changes in these areas?

What red flags, if any, do you feel you need to discuss with your future mate?

Think of a couple you know whose lifelong commitment you admire. What has their relationship taught you?

What two things concern you about giving up the single life?

What three things most excite you about entering married life?

What About Us?

Here are some important questions to discuss together:
- In what ways have you made decisions together in the past? How do you hope to make decisions together in the future?
- Are you both physically, financially, and emotionally free from previous relationships, including parents, dating partners, exes, and prior fiancé(e)s?
- Do you both have your families' blessings for your marriage? If not, who opposes it and why?
- Have you set a date for the wedding? What issues need to be resolved before that date?
- Once you're married, how will you respect the interests you don't share? (For example, maybe one of you loves traveling, but your future mate prefers staying close to home. Perhaps one of you enjoys dining out, but your fiancé(e) sees eating out as a frivolous expense. How will you resolve these differences?)

Just for Fun!

Take turns completing the following statements about your future mate. It's okay if you don't know every answer. Just use the opportunity to learn something new about each other.

Your birthday is _____.

Your favorite dessert is _____.

Your favorite pastime is _____.

Your favorite movie is _____.

You grew up in the town of _____.

In college, you majored in _____.

Politically, you usually vote _____ (conservative, liberal, moderate).

What Does God Say?

Read the following scriptures from Genesis that reveal God's purpose for marriage:

> Then God said, "Let us make man in our image, in our likeness, and let them rule over the fish of the sea and the birds of the air, over the livestock, over all the earth, and over all the creatures that move along the ground."

> So God created man in his own image,
>   in the image of God he created him;
>   male and female he created them. (Genesis 1:26–27)

> The LORD God said, "It is not good for the man to be alone. I will make a helper suitable for him." (Genesis 2:18)

3

SURVIVING OR THRIVING

How Do You Meet Each Other's Needs?

I [Dale] breathed in the crisp, cool air. It was an amazingly beautiful day for skiing, a time to reflect on my relationship with Susan and assess where our future might lead. That day I pondered what it was that drew me to her. As I stood alone on a mountaintop with the wind and sun in my face, I realized why I loved her so deeply.

Among the many reasons was that Susan met my deepest needs for sincere love and affection, for honesty and openness, and for a relationship with a godly woman. Our conversations were deep and real, and I knew I could trust my heart to her.

I felt that I could understand and meet her needs too. I knew that much of her life had been marred by dishonesty, financial insecurity, and a lack of commitment, and I firmly believed I could fill those needs. And I sure admired her. Most of all, though, I realized that God had been guiding both of us to know each other's needs and to learn how to meet them in practical and fulfilling ways.

Years later, meeting each other's needs has become a daily habit. Whether it's a back rub after a long day (which I appreciate), a quiet conversation by the fireplace (which she enjoys), an honest admission of falling short, or a hard day of working in the yard together, Susan and I have found ways to fulfill our personal and relational needs.

Still, there are times when we make mistakes or when one of us has a need that the other either doesn't know how to meet or isn't responsible to meet. We've come to realize that some needs can only be met by God Himself, and we understand that perfect love and unconditional acceptance can only be found by having a relationship with Him. So when circumstances are out of your control and you feel afraid or helpless, remember that only God can give you a peace that "transcends all understanding" (Philippians 4:7).

The objective of this chapter is to help you identify the needs you and your future spouse have, discern what wants and desires you may confuse as real needs, and help you better understand how to meet each other's needs. And working hard each and every day to meet those needs when you can will make your marriage a rewarding adventure.

NEEDS VERSUS WANTS

It's a tough job to sort out the difference between a personal want and a real need. The marketing media says you "need" to have everything they advertise, and you "need" it now. From makeup to perfume to new gadgets or a new car, commercials, billboards, and advertisements of all kinds shout to us that unless we have what they offer us, our "needs" won't be met, and we won't be successful. Yet although these are just marketing ploys to prompt us to buy things, we often get confused and think that what we want or desire is really what we need.

James and Laura looked like the perfect urban-chic couple. But behind closed doors, Laura's out-of-control spending was becoming an increasing frustration for James. Laura's closet contained thousands of dollars worth of name-brand shoes, the latest trendy fashions, and a vast array of glamour accessories. But James's home office was no better. All the latest high-tech toys cluttered his desk. He'd lined the walls with expensive artwork and bought high-priced furnishings to fill the room. James's tendency to splurge on things he wanted soon became a source of tension between him and Laura.

To others, James and Laura appeared to be the epitome of success, but beneath the facade, a storm was brewing—a storm of financial ruin from their gotta-have-it-all-now mentality. It wasn't until they nearly divorced because of the stress their deep debt had caused in their relationship that they finally figured out how to learn to meet real needs and let go of their many wants.

You might read this story and think, *Well, they were spending all of their money on wants, not needs!* And you'd be right. But it's easy to get caught up in wanting instant gratification. In fact, many couples are just like James and Laura. Understand that we're not saying all wants are bad. But making healthy decisions for your marriage will often require setting aside wants in order to meet legitimate needs.

That's why it's important to identify what your needs are now (as individuals and as a couple). But that's only half the job. Choosing daily to learn how to unselfishly meet each other's needs and giving grace when one of you falls short is the other critical component. We'll talk more about this in the "Take Action!" section of this chapter.

UNIVERSAL NEEDS

God knows exactly how He wired each of us and what our unique needs are. He also gave us universal needs. First, we need Him. He can help us understand ourselves and our mates. He can also guide us in knowing how to meet each other's deepest needs.

Second, we need each other. Marriage is the most intimate relationship of all. You can't be a loner or emotionally withdrawn without it adversely affecting your spouse. God created us to need each other, and when we understand His plan for us, we'll become the helpers for our mates that He created us to be.

Third, we have personal needs that are physical, emotional, spiritual, and social. The problem is that like James and Laura, we often get mixed up as to what's really an important and valid need, what's a selfish desire, and what's just something we think we want because it's been imposed on us by influences

Ask the Expert

In his classic book on marriage *His Needs, Her Needs*, Willard Harley says that the top five needs of men and women are different:

Men need

- Sexual fulfillment
- Companionship
- An attractive spouse
- Domestic support
- Admiration

Women need

- Affection
- Communication
- Honesty
- Financial support
- Family commitment

According to Harley, "The husband and wife who commit themselves to meet each other's needs will lay a foundation for lifelong happiness in marriage that is deeper and more satisfying than they ever dreamed possible."[1] He encourages each spouse to identify the other's deepest needs and do whatever it takes to make that partner satisfied and happy. Though your list of needs may not be exactly the same as Harley's, his book can help you understand the needs men and women have in a marriage relationship.

such as the media, peers, and family. And all too often, we expect, even demand, that all our needs and wants be met—especially by our spouses.

Mark and Gail confused each other constantly. From early in their marriage, Mark thought the only time he needed to be affectionate with Gail was when they were going to have sex. But Gail longed for nonsexual affection, and when she didn't get those needs met, she pulled away from Mark sexually. The more this happened, the more time Mark wanted to spend with his single friends, and the more Gail felt neglected. Then Gail refused to show Mark appreciation for his work or admiration for the things he did for her. In turn, Mark stopped affirming Gail for all she did and began withdrawing emotionally from her.

Although they loved each other deeply, as time passed, both partners began to feel frustrated and lonely. Finally they sat down with their pastor and talked about how they were both feeling. Their pastor pointed out that they were no longer meeting each other's needs, and he helped Mark and Gail get out of the vicious cycle they were in and back into a healthy cycle of serving each other.

Unmet needs can cause a lot of frustration, misunderstanding, and conflict in a relationship, especially in marriage.

MORE ABOUT WANTS

Beyond wanting material things, we also have selfish wants and desires that masquerade as needs. We may think we have the right to have our own needs (or wants) met first. We may think we need to be in control or have others do things our way, so we make demands, dominate our partners, or manipulate situations to get our needs met. We think we deserve to have a good time even when we can't afford it, to see an inappropriate movie even when it goes against our morals, or even to check out a porn site, thinking it's no big deal. And sometimes we don't even realize that those selfish desires can lead to addictions and other destructive habits that may alienate our families or destroy our marriages.

Sometimes the Holy Spirit will convict us of a destructive desire, but often other people, especially our loved ones, may point out our shortcomings. Even though it's not always easy, we should be humble enough to recognize that we may have a negative pattern of behavior, be grateful for the input, and choose to change.

Unless you understand the difference between a want or desire and a valid need, it's likely that you and your future mate will continually struggle to understand how you can be fulfilled, healthy, and whole as individuals and as a couple.

Take some time to think of five "wants" you have at the moment. Your list might include cars, houses, wedding-related items, vacation trips, and so on. Share your lists with each other. Again, not all wants are wrong or unhealthy. The key is to set healthy, positive priorities and to be realistic regarding what you want and what you need.

More About Needs

We all have basic human needs, such as the need for food and water, clothing, shelter, and safety. Meeting these physical needs contributes to our health and safety. But we also have emotional needs, such as the need to feel accepted, loved, valued, needed, and supported. And even though we're all different, to some extent we have social needs, such as having a sense of belonging, enjoying sexual intimacy with our spouses, and maintaining same-sex friendships.

How can you be sure you know and are meeting your future mate's deepest and most important needs? And frankly, whose needs come first?

Philippians 2:3–4 says, "Do nothing out of selfish ambition or vain conceit, but in humility consider others better than yourselves. Each of you should look not only to your own interests, but also to the interests of others." What do we learn from this verse? Our attitudes and the choices we make really do matter. This scripture encourages us to have a servant's heart, to have an unselfish determination to serve our mates. Whenever two people choose to selflessly serve each other, they experience peace, contentment, and satisfaction in their relationship.

However, think back to macho man Steve and his wife, Amy, in chapter 2. They're an example of a relationship in which one person is always giving and the other is always taking. It's important for both partners in a relationship to serve each other; without this, one person will begin to feel like a doormat, taken for granted and unappreciated. We want to help you understand that you *both* have needs that will have to be met, and you must work together to fulfill those needs.

There are two areas we want to concentrate on in this section: spiritual needs and emotional needs. Why? Because these two areas are often the toughest to understand, assess, and adjust to in a new marriage.

Spiritual Needs

We've mentioned that all of us were created to have a relationship with God. Without that relationship, we're missing a huge piece of life's puzzle. God has purposefully given us that need, and by fostering a close relationship with Him, we can learn to better handle our relationships with our loved ones and friends.

On a deep and real level, when you marry, you become one with your mate, and that has a spiritual reality to it. Whether or not you recognize it, you long to be spiritually connected to each other, and unless you cultivate that connection, there will always be an emptiness, an unfulfilled part of your relationship.

From the very beginning, Dale and I [Susan] determined to make our relationship a spiritual one and to develop our Christian walk together. I had been a Christian for more than 25 years, so prayer and Bible reading were part of my daily life. Dale was just beginning to deepen his relationship with the Lord, so at first it was a little difficult for him to pray aloud with me. Yet as we pressed on, Dale found a level of comfort and ease in praying together.

Now his prayers are intimate and real, as if he's talking to his closest Friend, and I enjoy every time we pray together.

We decided early on in our relationship that we needed to be intentional about growing spiritually as a couple and working together to meet our spiritual needs. We started by attending church together and finding time to discuss God's Word. And we joined a wonderful small group with couples who are real and transparent and with whom we can grow spiritually and relationally. All of these actions are part of meeting our spiritual needs as a couple.

What are your spiritual needs, and how can each of you meet those needs? You can meet these needs by first committing to grow together spiritually and developing a plan for what that will look like in your marriage. Do you attend church together regularly? If not, now is the time to find a church and get plugged in. Regular church attendance provides a time and place to worship together and an opportunity to be part of a community of believers. Participating together in ministry opportunities is another way to grow in your faith as a couple. You might look into service opportunities through your church or your community center. Consider serving at a soup kitchen or donating unused items to a shelter.

After you marry, attend a Bible study or a small group with other newly married couples with whom you can "do life." If your current church doesn't have a group, consider starting one.

Second, learn to pray together. For some couples, this isn't easy. If you haven't developed a pattern of praying together, start by saying a prayer before meals. As you become more comfortable praying aloud together, you can learn to pray at other times, such as when someone is struggling with an issue, when you're traveling, when you need to know God's will and His plan for your marriage, and so on. Dale and I enjoy our spiritual intimacy so much that we pray every morning when we get up, every evening before we go to sleep, and before each meal.

Third, consider asking an older married couple, whom you respect, to mentor you. Meet with that couple every few weeks or monthly. Be honest, transparent, and inquisitive. Ask them how to deal with issues you're encountering. Seek their advice regarding struggles you may have, and allow them to hold you accountable in those areas.

Maintaining your covenant commitment to God and to each other may not always be easy, but choosing daily to develop your walk with God as a couple can give your relationship a lasting foundation. Finally, realize that as

What Are Your Spiritual Needs?

Take a few minutes to talk about your different spiritual backgrounds. Here are some questions to get you started:

- Was church attendance a regular part of your childhood?
- On a scale of one to five (one being the least involvement; five being the most involvement) rate the level of church involvement you prefer.
- When you're married, would you like to pray before meals? At other times?
- How important is Bible reading to you? Is joining a Bible study with others something you would like to do?
- How important is spiritual leadership to you? Do you believe husbands should be the spiritual leaders of the home, or do you believe that both of you, working together, should lead your family spiritually?
- What religious traditions and/or doctrines are important to you? Baptism, Communion, church membership, evangelism, Christmas, Easter?

you grow and mature spiritually, your needs will change. Just as life is ever changing, so is your spiritual life.

Emotional Needs

Because emotional needs are deep and often intangible, you should assess as best you can what they are and whether they are realistic. Once you figure that out, you can express those needs to your future mate, and help him or her learn how to meet them, understanding that, as we said earlier, you can't expect him or her to meet all of your needs.

Sometimes you can explain the reasons for your emotional needs so your future spouse understands why you have those needs in the first place. When I [Susan] explained to Dale that my need for emotional safety stemmed from my past experiences with abuse, Dale compassionately desired to find every way possible to make me feel safe with him. When I learned how unappreciated Dale had felt in past relationships, I made a conscious decision to make sure I let him know how much I appreciate everything he does for me. Understanding the underlying feelings, experiences, pain, and scars that created his needs helped me to be purposeful about meeting them.

How do you do this? Once you recognize an emotional need you have, such as a need for safety, trust, or validation, think about the *why* behind your feelings. Maybe it's just your personality; maybe you've been hurt in the past; maybe you struggle with insecurity or self-esteem issues. Be open about sharing the reason with your future mate.

The truth is, your emotional needs will change over time (just like your spiritual needs). There will also be seasons in your marriage when you'll need to sacrifice some of your own needs for the good of your spouse or to strengthen your relationship. When you choose to do this, your relationship will deepen and become stronger through the trials of life. Respecting your husband, even when he doesn't deserve it, and loving your wife, even when it's not comfortable or convenient, are two tangible ways to make that happen.

TAKE ACTION! ASSESSING YOUR REAL NEEDS

We've established that everyone has some basic, intrinsic needs, but to differing degrees. I [Susan] need affection, honesty, and security; Dale needs appreciation, commitment, and good communication. We both need acceptance, affirmation, and a sense of being wanted, valued, needed, understood, and so much more.

What about each of you? Take some time to review the following list of needs and assess how important each need is to you individually on a scale of one to five (one being the least important; five being the most important). Though some of the categories may overlap, the words will trigger different feelings. This will help each of you understand your most important needs and those of your future spouse. Once you've assessed what each other's needs are, we'll discuss practical ways you can meet them.

I Need to Feel . . .	His	Hers
That I'm a priority	____	____
That we're a team	____	____
Accepted	____	____
Wanted	____	____
Needed	____	____
Understood	____	____
Appreciated	____	____
Supported	____	____

I Need . . .	His	Hers
Affection	____	____
Time alone	____	____
Regular communication	____	____
Romance	____	____

I Need . . .	His	Hers
Tenderness	_____	_____
Respect	_____	_____
Financial security	_____	_____
Safety	_____	_____
Trust	_____	_____
Dependability	_____	_____
Honesty	_____	_____
Companionship	_____	_____
Patience	_____	_____
Forgiveness	_____	_____
Commitment	_____	_____
Faithfulness	_____	_____
Sexual fulfillment	_____	_____
Validation	_____	_____
Reassurance	_____	_____
Approval	_____	_____
Encouragement	_____	_____
Quality time together	_____	_____

Take time to look over each other's ratings. Sometimes understanding and recognizing that your future mate has a need is enough to spark action. But at other times, your fiancé(e) may have no idea where to begin or how to meet your needs in a particular area. For example, perhaps your future mate rated romance as a strong need in her life. What does that mean to you? What does that mean to her? Maybe she appreciates flowers, phone calls throughout the day, love notes, and so on.

Maybe your fiancé indicated that he needs to feel as though the two of you are a team. This could mean he'd like for you to discuss important issues and make decisions together. Maybe he'd like for you to show interest in home projects or planning vacations.

Learning to meet each other's needs may come naturally in some areas, but if some areas are difficult, don't be afraid to talk about your feelings. If you're not sure how you can meet a need your spouse has mentioned, ask for examples. Take notes. Meeting each other's needs is an ongoing learning process. And remember, no one's perfect. There will be times when you'll disappoint your future spouse, and he or she will disappoint you. The goal is to keep working at your relationship, extend grace to each other, and be willing to communicate your needs to each other.

What About Me?

It's time to assess your individual needs in the following areas: spiritual, physical, emotional, social, financial, sexual, and intellectual. In each of these areas, list three needs you have.

Here are a few ideas to get you started:

- *Spiritually*—I need to have and maintain a personal relationship with God. I need to make my decisions based on ethical and moral values.
- *Physically*—Fitness, health, and attractiveness are important to me.
- *Emotionally*—I need to feel accepted, needed, and understood.
- *Socially*—I need time with same-sex friends, a sense of belonging, support, accountability, and companionship. Recreational companionship is important to me.
- *Financially*—I need enough money to feel a measure of security.
- *Sexually*—I need fulfillment, satisfaction, faithfulness, intimacy, and a sense of oneness.
- *Intellectually*—I need to continue to learn to be wise and successful.

What About Us?

Take turns naming three needs from the previous exercise that you think your future mate might not recognize as needs you have. Discuss how you can meet each other's needs in practical ways. Name three specific things you can start doing now.

Just for Fun!

What one talent do you wish you had?

So far, what has been your greatest accomplishment in life?

What Does God Say?

Isaiah 58:11 says, "The LORD will guide you always; he will satisfy your needs in a sun-scorched land." When your future mate fails to meet a need you have, God is able to meet it . . . whether He chooses to or not.

And sometimes you have to set aside your own needs to love another person. John 15:12–13 says, "My command is this: Love each other as I have loved you. Greater love has no one than this, that he lay down his life for his friends."

Even when you don't feel your needs are being met, remember Philippians 4:19: "My God will meet all your needs according to his glorious riches in Christ Jesus."

4

GREAT EXPECTATIONS

What Should You Expect in Your Marriage?

When Crystal and Andy married, Crystal thought she'd finally have the family she'd always dreamed of. After all, Andy was her best friend, her confidant, her everything. She expected that they'd enjoy a fairy-tale marriage in which they'd spend romantic evenings by the fire, enjoy long intimate discussions, and experience lots of love and joy.

But a few months after they married, Andy got a promotion that required him to work and travel extensively. He was thrilled with this opportunity, but Crystal wasn't so pleased. Left alone in the new city they moved to, Crystal felt confused, frustrated, and disappointed. When she tried to talk with Andy about her feelings, he became defensive. He felt like he couldn't please anyone—his wife or his boss—but he had no intention of passing up this new position. As time went on, their marriage eroded into anything but a fairy tale.

What happened? Crystal entered the marriage thinking that life would be perfect and that Andy would always strive to make her happy. Andy expected Crystal to be encouraging and supportive of his career, realizing that his advancement would benefit both of them.

We all have expectations for marriage. These come from your past experiences, your current circumstances, and even your dreams and goals for the future. Knowing how these expectations affect your life and how they can affect your relationship with your future mate, for good or bad, is important to the health of your marriage. Having expectations isn't necessarily a bad thing. You should expect your future mate to treat you with respect and vice versa. And you both should expect to be physically and emotionally faithful to each other.

In fact, God has expectations too. As we mentioned earlier, God expects you to leave your family of origin and bond to the one He gives you as your mate (Genesis 2:24). He expects you and your spouse to become one, to find true companionship, to experience real intimacy, and to reflect His glory in your relationship. He expects you to serve each other unselfishly; accept one another's unique personalities, needs, and differences; and honor your covenant with each other. He also expects you to love each other, be merciful and forgiving, and be patient as you learn and grow together.

When Dale and I [Susan] started to get serious about our relationship, we decided to explore the area of expectations, especially since we were older and more set in our ways. Many evenings were devoted to discussing what we expected in a marriage. These talks covered all kinds of topics, from emotional safety to kids to praying together on a regular basis.

As you begin to explore your expectations for marriage, you won't discover all of the expectations you and your future mate have in every area of life, but it won't take long before you realize how comfortable or uncomfortable you might be with each other's expectations.

THE BASICS

Often we don't even realize what expectations we may have of ourselves or others or even understand where they came from.

Where do we get most of our expectations?

1. *Our family of origin* affects us greatly. For good or bad, our parents are usually our most influential role models. Our siblings influence us too.

2. *Our peers* have a huge influence on what we expect of relationships, especially during the teen and young-adult years.

3. *Our culture*—especially the entertainment industry and the media—has a tremendous influence on our expectations of marriage and relationships.

Leann and Randy grew up with very different ways of working in the kitchen. Randy was raised in a military home where you cleaned as you prepared the meal, everything spic-and-span and sanitary. Leann was a whirlwind when she cooked, happily creating a messy hurricane of pots, pans, and utensils. She left cupboard doors open and clutter on the kitchen counters. All of this drove Randy crazy. After a few years of frustration, the two struck a compromise: Leann prepared the food, and Randy tidied up after her. Their nightly tradition of cooking dinner together helped them have time to talk and catch up on their days.

Was either of them wrong in their expectations? No. Their expectations resulted from their different home lives. At first they both assumed that the way each of them did things was the best way. Fortunately, they were wise enough to compromise and not let their different expectations damage their relationship.

It's important for both of you to understand how appropriate or realistic your expectations are regarding your future mate and your marriage. Most likely, many of your expectations aren't wrong; they're just different. But not knowing what is expected can result in conflict, stress, and frustration.

Let's take a closer look at unrealistic and realistic expectations.

UNREALISTIC EXPECTATIONS

One of the things my roommates and I [Susan] enjoyed doing together as single women was watching chick flicks. But that was problematic. Hollywood often promotes unrealistic, even false, expectations of what a relationship should look like, how we should treat the opposite sex, how we should conduct ourselves in a relationship, what we should expect in a marriage, and so much more. Fortunately, since all my roomies were Christians, we often discussed the media's fabrications versus God's expectations for relationships and marriage.

Movies, music, TV, radio, the Internet, books, and magazines often portray relationships and marriage as temporary, shallow, deceptive, replaceable, and unfulfilling. Too often we unconsciously digest the wrong messages, and our expectations are formed from distorted views of relationships. Consequently, we develop unrealistic expectations for our relationship with our future mate.

Which of the following unrealistic messages about relationships have you absorbed, even unconsciously, from the media?

- Relationships aren't meant to last.
- Wealth and material things bring happiness.
- Sexual experimentation is necessary in order to know a person.
- Cohabitation before marriage is healthy.
- Violence and sensuality is entertaining.

Unfortunately, we've acquired other unrealistic expectations from our culture. Our society often glorifies the individual, encourages personal fulfillment—even to the detriment of others—and discourages sacrifice and selflessness.

Matthew and Julie expected to have a healthy marriage, but unfortunately, they didn't have a very realistic understanding of what that meant. Julie expected Matthew to just "know" what she wanted or expected. She regularly got offended or upset when Matthew didn't meet her needs, and even though she knew she was being rather selfish, she demanded her way more often than not.

Matthew was surprised that they argued about little things, and their constant fighting made him feel insecure about their relationship. Meanwhile, instead of articulating their concerns, Matthew and Julie just kept getting more and more frustrated that the other didn't meet his or her expectations. They didn't seek help to break this cycle of fighting and frustration, so it continued.

Look over the following list and consider whether you've been influenced by any of these faulty assumptions:

- We'll live happily ever after.
- Marriage is always a 50-50 proposition.
- I'll be complete and fulfilled in marriage.
- Marriage will solve most of my problems.
- Nothing will ever change in our relationship.
- We'll never argue or disagree.
- Differences don't really matter.
- Sex will always be great.
- I'll always feel in love.

Choose two or three of the assumptions and talk about why they aren't realistic. For example, can a relationship always be 50-50? What if, as Dale and I [Susan] experienced, you encounter illnesses or trials? Could there be times when one of you has to rely more heavily on the other?

Understanding each other's expectations—the realistic as well as the not-so-realistic—will make for a smoother, stronger marriage. Now let's look at realistic expectations.

REALISTIC EXPECTATIONS

Becky and Thom spent much of their engagement period discussing their expectations and how they would split up daily duties and chores. They talked about their individual goals, dreams, interests, hobbies, and career plans. Before they said "I do," Becky had clearly communicated that she didn't want to be responsible for cooking dinner every night of the week, so they agreed that they would each take two nights a week to cook a sit-down meal at home. Since they both valued and recognized the importance of intentionally and regularly setting aside time to build their relationship, they also designated Friday night for their weekly date night.

Ask the Expert

In his book *Starved for Affection*, Dr. Randy Carlson writes,

> When we get married, we assume and expect that our spouse knows how to love us. I used to think that, but after years of working with people, I realize this is unfair because no one is a mind reader. Unless you share with your spouse how you need to be loved, he or she can't know it. I talk to guys who don't have a clue how to love their wives and to women who don't know how to love their husbands. Both of you must tell each other how to connect. When do you feel closest to your spouse? When do you share emotionally? . . . Let your spouse know this crucial information.[1]

Dr. Carlson's book discusses our need for affection in marriage. Whether you're a "head person" (intellectual and factual), a "heart person" (a feeler), or a "hand person" (one who serves and does things for others), meeting your spouse's multidimensional need for affection is important. Men and women have differences in this area, and Dr. Carlson explains why we need affection to feel loved, how to get it despite our differences, and why it's so important in marriage.

Becky and Thom also discussed long-term goals. Thom supported and encouraged Becky in her career, but he also wanted to make sure she had the option to stay home or work part-time when they had children. Becky agreed that she wanted to be the primary caregiver for their children. These expectations directly influenced the decisions they made regarding vehicles, housing, their household budget, and education during the first few months and years of their marriage.

Each of you has goals, dreams, and expectations, and they may be very different from your future mate's. This is normal and expected. The solution to merging these expectations successfully is communication, compromise, and care. Do you hope to get your graduate degree? Do you dream of traveling to another country? Is furthering your career very important to you? Do you expect your mate to support you in realizing your hopes and dreams? Take a few minutes to talk about individual goals and aspirations.

We all seek happiness, but how we achieve it varies from person to person. This is another area where expectations come into play. What is fun for one person may not be fun for the other. Do you expect your future spouse to watch sports on television with you? Maybe you enjoy gardening and expect your future mate to help you with the yard work. Maybe your fiancé(e) enjoys hiking, while you would rather browse in a local bookstore. It's okay to have different interests.

Before Dale and I [Susan] married, Dale was used to taking a dozen or more ski trips each winter. I was a bit concerned I'd end up the wife of a ski bum, spending lots of evenings alone waiting for him to come home from a day on the mountain. More than that, the thought of being physically hurt myself made me afraid to ski with him, and though Dale understood my concerns, after we married he encouraged me to join him and give it a try. At first I wasn't willing to leave my comfort zone (which wasn't on the slopes!). Eventually, though, I decided to take the risk, not only to be with my husband but also to understand his passion for the sport. To my surprise, I discovered I actually liked it—after the fifth try—and I learned a valuable lesson: I needed to be more willing to try new things, especially if they would bring us closer together and allow us to enjoy special moments, such as basking in the wonder of the snow-capped Rocky Mountain peaks.

Take turns naming at least three forms of entertainment each of you especially enjoys. Of these activities, which three would you enjoy doing as a couple?

Which would you prefer not doing together?

FAMILY EXPECTATIONS

One of the greatest aspects of marriage, and sometimes one of the biggest surprises or uncertainties of your journey together, relates to having children. What are your expectations about having and raising children? Discussing your feelings about starting a family is vital to preparing for your lifelong adventure together. What if children come earlier than you planned . . . or not at all?

Kelly came from a family of eight and loved having so many brothers and sisters. Her fiancé, Robert, however, was an only child. Soon after the honeymoon, Kelly began talking about starting a family. Robert was shocked. He had assumed that they'd wait several years before having children. Even then, he had no intention of having more than two.

Talking about such issues as having children might seem premature right now. You might be thinking about the wedding and feeling excited about starting your life together. Maybe you're assuming that your future mate feels the same way you do. But just as Robert and Kelly discovered, that's a dangerous assumption.

So let's take a few moments to address this important topic. Read the following questions and take turns answering aloud.

- Do you expect to have children? If so, how many?
- Do you believe that not having children is a legitimate lifestyle choice? Why or why not?
- How do you feel about birth control?
- If we have children, who will be the primary caregiver? Would one of us become a stay-at-home parent? How do you feel about that?
- What if we're unable to have children? How would you feel about fertility treatments?
- How do you feel about adoption? Would you consider it if we couldn't have children?
- When would you like to start a family? Within the first two years of marriage? In five or more years?
- Should we budget for the future with children in mind?

Tips for a Strong Marriage

Here are some tips for meeting each other's expectations and making your future marriage strong:

- When you discover that one or both of you have conflicting expectations, choose to solve the problem as a team.
- Expect that commitment and compromise mean giving in sometimes. Compromise is the operative word.
- Be flexible. You don't have to be stuck in the way you've always done something. Find new ways that work for both of you.
- Make decisions based on what's best for the two of you.
- Set reasonable goals, make plans, and dream together.

Looking back over the questions you just answered, which ones, if any, did the two of you get stuck on? Which couldn't you reach a compromise on? Did you see a particular issue differently? If so, talk with a pastor, mentor, or counselor about the issue. Make sure you resolve your differences before going further in your relationship.

Because we're distinctly different from each other in more ways than we're the same, we must understand each other's expectations if we're to have a healthy relationship. And because unknown or unexpressed expectations can often lead to trouble, it takes a lot of work to communicate your expectations and then understand your future mate's expectations of you and your relationship.

What About Me?

We mentioned that our backgrounds often influence our expectations. Think of two or three ways your family of origin has affected your marriage expectations.

What are your expectations regarding the following topics?
- Where would you like to live?
- How would you like to spend your free time together?
- How much personal/alone time do you need?
- How much sleep do you need? Are you a morning or evening person?
- How often do you expect to visit extended family?
- Do you expect to be very social as a couple? To spend much time with friends?
- Do you expect to take family vacations every year?
- Do you plan to make a career change after you get married?
- How often do you expect to have sex?

What About Us?

Look back over the list of questions in the previous section. In what areas did your expectations conflict? What questions did you answer similarly? In those areas where you answered differently, talk about ways you can compromise.

Just for Fun!

Describe your idea of a perfect date. Where would you go? What would you do? What would the weather be like?

What Does God Say?

Godly expectations come from a heart and mind that seek to be like the Lord. As we understand what He expects of us, we can learn to expect godly things from ourselves and others. Second Peter 1:3–8 is a great place to start:

> His divine power has given us everything we need for life and godliness through our knowledge of him who called us by his own glory and goodness. Through these he has given us his very great and precious promises, so that through them you may participate in the divine nature and escape the corruption in the world caused by evil desires.
>
> For this very reason, make every effort to add to your faith goodness; and to goodness, knowledge; and to knowledge, self-control; and to self-control, perseverance; and to perseverance, godliness; and to godliness, brotherly kindness; and to brotherly kindness, love. For if you possess these qualities in increasing measure, they will keep you from being ineffective and unproductive in your knowledge of our Lord Jesus Christ.

Here are a few other scriptures that will help you develop healthy relationships:

We take captive every thought to make it obedient to Christ. (2 Corinthians 10:5)

Do not be deceived: God cannot be mocked. A man reaps what he sows. The one who sows to please his sinful nature, from that nature will reap destruction. (Galatians 6:7–8)

Do not love the world or anything in the world. (1 John 2:15)

BEAUTIFULLY DIFFERENT

Can Your Differences Be Gifts from God?

Two of our closest friends, Pam and Ben, make beautiful music together. But the individual sounds they make are very different. Ben has a high tenor voice, and Pam has a strong and lovely alto voice. Opposites, yes. Different, for sure. But because they've learned how to blend their different voices and adjust their unique sounds so one doesn't overpower the other, their music is memorable and pleasing.

That's the way it should be with a husband and wife. The way God made you as a man and a woman can be a blessing in disguise. Sure, there may be times when you find your differences a mystery— even a bit weird—but they can be the things you can appreciate as God's creativity (Genesis 1:27; 2:22–23).

Your differences can also bring balance to your individual lives. Sometimes we get myopic, seeing our way of doing things as the *only* way, thinking our way is the *right* way. But adjusting your thinking so that you appreciate your differences can keep you humble and unselfish and can help you grow and mature as individuals and as a couple.

Just look around and see how differently God made everything, from snowflakes and fingerprints to you and your future spouse. Some of these differences probably attracted you to each other initially, but the truth is that when you live with those differences 24-7, they can sometimes become frustrating, confusing, and exasperating.

Before Johanna and Paul were married, they wondered why newlyweds argued over which way to roll the toilet paper or the proper way to squeeze a tube of toothpaste. Those trivialities seemed so petty to them. But soon they realized how differences can become such a big deal in marriage.

Laundry was never at the top of Johanna's list of favorite household chores, and Paul wasn't impressed with her creative laundry shortcuts. After her first load of laundry, Paul said, "I appreciate you doing the laundry, *but* I don't like the way you fold my T-shirts."

Johanna hissed back, "They're just T-shirts. What's the big deal?" As she stormed off, she thought, *He can fold his own precious T-shirts!*

Without a doubt, like Johanna and Paul, you'll encounter differences that will frustrate you. And you'll have to figure out how to deal with each situation. After two T-shirt-folding lessons from Paul and a slice of humble pie for Johanna, they finally worked out their laundry differences. Johanna decided that she could learn to fold Paul's T-shirts the way he liked them, and now they laugh at the memory of this simple difference.

Working through your differences can deepen your relationship and bring you closer together. But it's not always as easy as learning a new way to fold T-shirts. Believe it or not, God has a plan and a purpose for creating each of you with those differences. He plans to use the differences each of you brings to the marriage to transform you so that you will complement each other.

Romans 12:4–6 says,

Just as each of us has one body with many members, and these members do not all have the same function, so in Christ we who are many form one body, and each member belongs to all the others. We have different gifts, according to the grace given us.

This passage of Scripture explains to us how the body of Christ is one body, made up of individuals who are very different from one another. If we view a married couple as being a microcosm of the body of Christ, we can see this connection even more clearly.

Don't forget that many times, neither of you is wrong; your ways of thinking or acting are just different. Take those differences and discover how they can actually strengthen your relationship.

Isabel and Sean were polar opposites. She was from Mexico; he was a third-generation Irishman. Although both grew up Catholic, their family traditions were very different. Her family enjoyed huge get-togethers; his family preferred small, intimate dinners. As a result of their upbringings, their cultural differences needed to be discussed so they could decide what they wanted to bring into their interracial marriage and how they'd deal with the family differences. Isabel brought some of her traditions into the marriage and left others behind, and so did Sean; both were better for it.

Although there are often challenges in marrying someone from a different background, as Isabel and Sean did, the positive cultural experiences can enlarge each of you through the years.

It's best to take a good look at your differences before you marry. Otherwise, you'll encounter some extra struggles and adjustments later. If either of you ignores or hides your different thoughts, attitudes, or actions, you could end up feeling betrayed, as though your mate has been deceiving you. Sooner or later those differences will surface and affect your relationship. Clearly communicating the differences you observe now—from how you set the table to how you worship on Sunday—and discussing how you can navigate them to make your relationship stronger can help you avoid problems later.

As we mentioned before, interfaith marriages can be very challenging. If you're a Christian, marrying a nonbeliever can lead to a plethora of marital struggles with values, morals, time, friendships, finances, and so much more. And as we saw earlier in 2 Corinthians 6:14, Scripture clearly states that this is something Christians should not do. Our recommendation is that if your fiancé(e) doesn't share your faith, step back and reevaluate your relationship. An evangelistic marriage (marrying someone who's not a believer in the hopes that he or she will become a Christian) rarely works well.

If you choose to continue your relationship, be open about your expectations in this area. Do you expect your future mate to respect your faith and the choices you make because of your beliefs? Is he or she willing to participate in religious traditions and holidays with you?

Interdenominational marriages, in which couples choose to stay in their separate denominations, bring their own challenges. Where will you go to church? How will you raise your children? Discuss these issues thoroughly and make a plan of action before you marry. If you can't come to a mutual decision, slow down and revisit your plans to marry.

In this chapter, we'll discuss how to negotiate gender differences, how your different life histories influence you, and how your personality differences may affect your relationship. We'll learn how to deal with those differences in healthy ways, and we'll see how God can use your differences to make you better people.

GENDER DIFFERENCES

As I [Susan] write this section, I'm in an airport watching several preschool boys and girls play. And from where I'm sitting, there's no doubt that these loud and aggressive boys are wired differently than the gentle and giggly girls. From a physical and cultural standpoint, it's not difficult to observe gender differences, even among toddlers. Psychologically, boys think differently than girls. So why are we surprised when a man and a woman fall in love and encounter myriad differences?

Your future mate will have certain strengths and gifts that you don't, and vice versa. In this way, men and women complement one another. While we agree and accept that all people are different and that there are exceptions to every general rule, women tend to be more emotional, social, interdependent, and ever changing. They need love and affirmation to feel secure and cared for. Women often express their feelings freely, listen with their emotions, and become personally invested in situations far more easily than men. Men, you can start to bridge this difference by sharing your time, thoughts, and feelings with your wives.

Dale is great at sharing his life with me, and he often does unexpected things to show he cares, such as preparing dinner, doing laundry, or planning a trip. His objective is to love me the way I am and meet my needs, even though they're different from his.

Men are often more logical than women, see things in generalities, and are goal oriented, which enables them to tackle tasks and solve problems well. They need to be respected for their unique traits as well as to feel loved. Because men are usually more visual, they need to be desired and know their wives are attractive and attracted to them. Women, you can begin to bridge this difference after you're married by treating your mates with respect, sharing intimacy freely with them, and doing little things to show you're interested in them sexually.

As you learn to appreciate each other's differences, you'll begin to see how you can be stronger and more effective as a couple. And having a good sense of humor about your differences can help you find joy in every situation.

BACKGROUND DIFFERENCES

Dale and I [Susan] experienced very different backgrounds. He came from a small, close-knit, Protestant family and grew up in Southern California. I grew up in a large, blended Catholic family in upstate New York, so our family experiences were quite different from each other's.

We also grew up more than a decade apart, so our generational differences also affect the way we think, feel, experience life, and relate to others. And that's okay. Although these differences could be viewed as barriers to our intimacy, they can also be seen as assets that bring well roundedness to our relationship.

Our attitudes and choices also form some of our differences. So do our culture and the society in which we live. Since I became a Christian by the time I was 20, my choices were more conservative than Dale's, and my attitudes reflected my Christian worldview. Dale's experiences in the military and secular society brought about some of the differences we've faced. Yet, as he's grown in his faith, his attitudes have changed, and so have our differences.

It's important to respect your differences and avoid the tendency to try to make your mate into who you think he or she should be. Respecting his or her choices is a good way to do this. Susan allowed me [Dale] to draw my own conclusions and make my own decisions regarding faith and other issues. For example, even while we were still dating, we discussed the possibility of my getting water baptized, but I wasn't ready. A few years into our marriage, a sermon prompted me to make the decision. Susan had given me the freedom to decide the better path to take when I was ready. She allowed the Lord to work on me rather than trying to do the work for Him.

If you'll honor each other's backgrounds, serve each other despite your differences, and value the lessons you've learned through life's experiences, you'll give each other grace when one of you makes a mistake, and you'll grow into a healthy couple.

PERSONALITY DIFFERENCES

Books galore have been written about the different personality types. There are introverts who marry extroverts, neatniks who marry slobs, and savers who marry spenders.

Mary was an extremely passive woman. She married an aggressive, controlling man who made life a daily challenge. Patti was a deeply spiritual person who married Gary, a casual Sunday churchgoer. And Alana married a serious athlete even though she cared little about sports. In all these situations, these couples struggled to deal with their major differences.

Whether you're an optimist and your fiancé(e) is a pessimist, or you're

Ask the Expert

Ephesians 5:22, 25 says, "Wives, submit to [respect] your husbands as to the Lord. . . . Husbands, love your wives, just as Christ loved the church and gave himself up for her."

More than anything, a man needs respect and a woman needs to feel loved. When these core needs are met, each partner is happier and the marriage is healthier. When either love or respect is lacking, couples tend to get caught up in an unhealthy cycle of treating each other poorly, and a lot of it has to do with communication—or the lack of it.

As Emerson Eggerichs wrote in his book *Love and Respect*,

The way I like to picture the difference between men and women [and how they communicate] is that the woman looks at the world through pink sunglasses that color all she sees. The man, however, looks at the world through blue sunglasses that color all he sees. Men and women can look at precisely the same situation and see life much differently. Inevitably, their pink and blue lenses cause their interpretation of things to be at odds to some degree.[1]

Eggerichs helps couples learn how to communicate so they can meet the most important needs of their spouse. If your marriage ever gets in an unhealthy cycle, or if you feel disrespected or unloved, Eggerichs's book can help you learn how to get back on track.

reserved and your future mate is spontaneous, or you're a talker and he's a reflective and quiet person, or you're a morning dove and she's a night owl, you can work out your differences through lovingly negotiating your interests, needs, and desires.

You might have to get creative about the ways you blend your differences. Instead of seeing your personality differences as major roadblocks, come up with ways to get around those differences. For example, a man who doesn't like to entertain can learn to enjoy having people over by using his barbecue skills; a woman who is an early bird can try to rearrange her schedule so she can participate in her husband's late-night activities. A spouse who doesn't play sports can learn how to keep score. Whatever compromise you make, there should be a balance so that one of you isn't doing all the flexing.

Recognize that some of your differences may actually be gifts. First Corinthians 12:4–6 says, "There are different kinds of gifts, but the same Spirit. There are different kinds of service, but the same Lord. There are different kinds of working, but the same God works all of them in all men."

Dale is very organized and meticulous, and that's a gift to me [Susan]. He naturally keeps well-organized drawers (which I hate doing) and pays the bills (which I hate doing even more). Although I could view his perfectionism as an irritation, I receive it as a gift from God. I, on the other hand, enjoy giving gifts, keeping up with correspondence, and entertaining guests. Dale could see these as nuisances that take time away from our time together, but instead, he's pleased that I use my gift of hospitality to keep up with our friends and families. It's all about the way you choose to view the differences you have.

WORKING OUT YOUR DIFFERENCES

Why do some differences between you and your future mate bug you so much? Do they make you feel like a failure, guilty, alienated, or offended? What causes those feelings? When something about your future mate bothers you, stop and think about the reason.

Once you understand the source of those negative feelings, you can either choose to let that irritation go or talk to your future spouse about it. Don't try to change or fix your future mate; let him or her choose to change. Or you can make the choice to let it go. Be humble enough to put your relationship before your own desires, habits, or differences.

When you have differences that really bug you, rather than focusing on the negative feelings you're experiencing, use the process of working through those differences and finding ways to overcome them as an opportunity to help you grow as a couple. Remember that your relationship is a journey, not a destination; it's an ongoing process that will take effort.

Focus on what caused you to fall in love in the first place—the good things, the fun things, the positive things. Focus on your loved one's strengths. Refuse to devalue each other's uniqueness. A critical spirit is a relationship killer. Judging, comparing, and rejecting the other person's different behavior will only cause defensiveness, insecurity, frustration, and hurt. Sometimes you need to choose to accept a difference rather than criticize it, and you may have to bite your tongue, even if it hurts.

Here are five simple steps to make your differences count:

1. *Remember.* It was probably your future spouse's differences that attracted you to each other in the first place. Think back to when your relationship was new, and remember why you liked these differences.

2. *Don't ignore differences.* Identify your differences and learn what makes your future spouse tick by studying his or her way of doing things. You might even discover that you like your spouse's way of doing something better than your way.

3. *Evaluate and negotiate.* Even though you're unique individuals, in some ways you may not really be that different from each other. Look for areas where you can find a middle ground, choose to grow in areas where you are different, and appreciate the things that come more naturally for your future spouse than for you.

That difference may even become a new area of common interest. But beware: if the difference is due to a bad habit, an unhealthy behavior, or a destructive pattern that will negatively affect your relationship, then you must set boundaries and understand those limits before you marry.

4. *Discover how God can use your differences.* You don't have to view your differences as incompatible or irreconcilable; you can choose to reconcile your differences and become compatible—even in spite of your differences.

5. *Embrace change.* Changing old habits and learning new things can be a positive experience. You might consider taking a class together or reading a book on a topic you often disagree about, such as money or communication. By learning from the same source, you're more likely to grow closer in this area. Keep in mind that the goal in marriage is unity, not sameness.

TAKING THE HIGH ROAD

How can Scripture help you take the high road in your relationship? Ephesians 4:2–3 says, "Be completely humble and gentle; be patient, bearing with one another in love. Make every effort to keep the unity of the Spirit through the bond of peace." By applying this verse to your everyday actions and words, you can make your differences work for you instead of against you.

1. Be humble. Instead of becoming defensive and pointing the finger at your future mate, evaluate your own motives and behavior first. Realize that your way of doing things may not always be the best way. Your future mate's way may not be, either. Sometimes it's best to work together to find a new way of folding your laundry or making your bed. When Dale and I [Susan] married, we folded towels two different ways, but Dale's son Erik showed us a third way, which we adopted because it worked best for us.

2. Be gentle. When a difference drives you crazy, don't manipulate or try to bring about change by shame or criticism. Instead, be gentle as you discuss the problem. Without acting frustrated or annoyed, Dale kindly convinced me [Susan] that rolling the toilet paper over the top was more efficient, and I was happy to oblige him, since it really didn't matter to me. Remember that differences are a part of the one you love, and your relationship is much more important than the way you do something.

3. Be patient. You're both on a lifelong journey of learning and growing together. It takes time to unlearn old habits and learn new ones. Although Susan works hard, she knows how to stop and enjoy life, but I [Dale] still have a hard time knowing when to quit working. Fortunately, Susan is patient with me, even when I don't know when to stop what I'm doing and spend time with her. Sometimes being patient means loving your spouse in spite of the differences.

4. Keep the unity and peace. Differences can make you feel disunited and steal the peace in your relationship, if you let them. Trust God's Spirit to help you find peace when differences threaten to tear you apart. This may mean taking some time alone to pray and calm down before you come together again to talk things through.

Differences can be a challenge, but they can also help you grow as individuals and as a couple like few things can. Embrace the challenge to find peace and contentment in the midst of your differences. After all, each of you is one of a kind; God made you that way!

What About Me?

As individuals, we all have unique personalities, qualities, and life experiences that make us different from others. Look at the following list of topics and write down ways you're different from your future spouse.

Family customs:

Education background:

Personality traits:

Communication style:

Favorite hobbies or interests:

What About Us?

You may discover that your differences are what make you successful as a couple. Answer the following questions about your individual strengths and weaknesses. After you've finished, review your answers and talk about the areas in which you balance or complement one another.

List five areas that you would consider your areas of strength. (For example: social skills, financial management, organization, patience, etc.)

His strengths:

Her strengths:

Now list five areas that you consider your areas of weakness. (For example: self-discipline, communicating feelings or needs, becoming easily angered, etc.)

His weaknesses:

Her weaknesses:

Just for Fun!

Which musical instrument best describes your personality and why?

What personality traits do you love most about your future mate?

What Does God Say?

Consider what God says about your differences:

> Do to others as you would have them do to you. (Luke 6:31)

> May the God who gives endurance and encouragement give you a spirit of unity among yourselves as you follow Christ Jesus, so that with one heart and mouth you may glorify the God and Father of our Lord Jesus Christ.
>
> Accept one another, then, just as Christ accepted you, in order to bring praise to God. (Romans 15:5–7)

There are different kinds of gifts, but the same Spirit. There are different kinds of service, but the same Lord. There are different kinds of working, but the same God works all of them in all men. (1 Corinthians 12:4–6)

You, my brothers, were called to be free. But do not use your freedom to indulge the sinful nature; rather, serve one another in love. (Galatians 5:13)

Be completely humble and gentle; be patient, bearing with one another in love. Make every effort to keep the unity of the Spirit through the bond of peace. (Ephesians 4:2–3)

6

LOVING COMMUNICATION

How Do You Express Love?

Communication is the lifeblood of any relationship. It will affect all other aspects of your marriage. By it you inform, explain, influence, and build intimacy with each other. Good communication is the act of revealing yourself—your past experiences, your present feelings, and your future dreams. It's sharing your feelings, fears, needs, and desires honestly, carefully, and with the right timing, tone, and attitude. It involves setting boundaries, confronting problems, and at times saying "I'm sorry."

It's best for a couple to establish positive communication habits early on. Most mornings when the alarm goes off—20 minutes before we actually need to get up—Susan and I [Dale] have a tradition of taking a few minutes of quiet time when we can be still, talk with each other about our plans for the day, and pray together.

We've also started another tradition that ends our day in a special way. Often, before we go to sleep, we simultaneously give each other foot rubs while we talk about our days and pray together. It's a time when we can relax and reconnect.

The fact is that life is busy for all of us, and we can easily get sidetracked by daily responsibilities. All too often we take our loved ones for granted. Outside pressures increase, and our closeness decreases. And the busier we are, the stronger the potential for poor communication with our future spouses. Susan and I have learned over time that we have to push the Pause button, be still, and listen to each other with love, attention, and respect in order to foster good communication in our marriage.

In chapter 1, we saw that 1 Corinthians 13:4–8 is our scriptural model for the best way to love one another:

> Love is patient, love is kind. It does not envy, it does not boast,
> it is not proud. It is not rude, it is not self-seeking, it is not easily
> angered, it keeps no record of wrongs. Love does not delight in
> evil but rejoices with the truth. It always protects, always trusts,
> always hopes, always perseveres.
>
> Love never fails.

What's love got to do with communication? Everything! At its best, communication is simply expressing love a thousand different ways, whether it's affirmation, encouragement, or admitting when we're wrong and humbly saying we're sorry. It's sharing thoughts and feelings verbally and nonverbally. Throughout this chapter, we'll look at the art of communication, and we'll see the best ways to express love through words—keeping in mind God's definition of love. We'll also look at the potential problems we can run into when communicating.

WHAT IS LOVING COMMUNICATION?

Loving communication is characterized by qualities such as patience, kindness, humility, honesty, and trust. We all have to consciously work on becoming loving communicators, but as Christians, we also have the help of the Holy Spirit, who produces His fruit in us (Galatians 5:22–23).

1. Patience. Communication isn't always easy. Sometimes you may struggle to make your points understood, and sometimes your disagreements may drive you crazy. So when working through misunderstandings and differences, patience is one of the most important keys to successful communication. When you choose to demonstrate patience through your attitudes, actions, and words, when you choose to walk your talk and be real and honest, and when you patiently allow your future mate to do the same, you'll have the basis you need to communicate effectively.

2. Kindness. Before we married, I [Susan] discovered a lump in my breast, and after much fear, worry, and a biopsy, I learned that it wasn't cancer. After we married, I did have cancer—and of all places, on the tip of my nose! That was a traumatic experience for me as a woman. What if I ended up disfigured from the surgery? Would Dale still love me? Thankfully, in both instances, Dale's kind words showed me love and support that were deeper and stronger than either medical crisis.

Choosing to use kind words to affirm, praise, support, and give feedback are only a few ways to create intimate communication between you and your future mate. The opposite behavior, rudeness, will destroy intimate communication. Even when you're in the midst of a conflict, you can still maintain the right heart attitude as you convey information, discuss difficult topics, and even vent, by consciously choosing your words and speaking with a kind and loving attitude. Yes, it takes restraint, but if you choose to be careful about what you say, you can succeed, even in the toughest situation.

Unfortunately, some people don't understand this, especially Darci. Every time we got together with her and her husband, Sam, Darci would make some snide, derogatory remark to or about him. "You know where that goes, Sam." "I've told you that before, Sam." Her words weren't the problem, though. It was her tone of voice, the way she cocked her head, the way she looked at him. Sam took the brunt of her unkind communication, but eventually, Darci's unkind words made us feel uncomfortable spending time around her.

You can show kindness by the warmth in your voice, a twinkle in your eye, a smile on your face, or a loving touch. Kimberly and Jay show this well. The way she looks at him, the gentle way he touches her arm as he passes her in the kitchen, the quick kiss they exchange before they get out of the car, and the midday e-mails they send while they're at work—all of these actions affirm, support, and communicate that each wants the other to be a part of his or her innermost life.

3. *Humility.* One young couple we counseled had a recurring problem. The extremely verbal wife tended to interrupt and talk over her husband. She often boasted about what she knew and spoke without considering how he might feel, even nagging about things she didn't like about him. After becoming aware of how her behavior affected her husband, she eventually learned to temper her tendency to talk all the time and was humbled in the process. Her husband, in turn, felt more safe and free to articulate his thoughts and feelings.

Pride demands that you be the center of attention—the know-it-all. It can cause people to monopolize conversations and not care about another person's needs or feelings. Pride can also cause people to interrupt, preach, nag, ignore others, invalidate another's feelings, and act as if they have all the answers. Proud people tend to blurt out whatever comes to mind, regardless of how those words might affect those listening. Have you ever met someone like this? We sure have.

It takes a humble heart to lovingly communicate. You have to be willing to listen instead of talk, to hear what the other person is really saying instead of monopolizing the conversation. Dale's father wisely said that you never learn anything new if you do all the talking.

4. *Selflessness.* You may sometimes get a little bit self-centered in your communication, think you should be the center of conversation, or forget that your future spouse has things to say and share. When communicating

with your future mate, try to set your own agenda aside for a minute, and in your desire to be heard be careful not to demand, push, manipulate, coerce, or make someone feel guilty for not doing what you want. God wants you to communicate your love to one another as you build each other up, praise one another's accomplishments, honor each other, affirm each other's positive traits, and give grace when the other makes mistakes.

5. *Honesty.* Little white lies, half-truths, exaggerations, fibs—anything that isn't truthful—is an enemy of good communication and destructive to your relationship. It can destroy trust so that your loved one can no longer believe what you say, and you may no longer feel free to communicate because you feel guilty and ashamed.

Sharon just loved to buy things, but her husband, Tony, tried to keep her on a budget. When something new "appeared" at the house, she told Tony that her friend gave it to her or she bought it on clearance. When the bills came in, Sharon made up more lies to cover her tracks, but Tony knew her stories couldn't be true.

Deception and secrecy are never the solutions to any problem you may face in your relationship. If you've ever been the victim of deception, like Dale and I [Susan] were in previous relationships, you know how damaging it can be. So choose to speak the truth in love—gently, lovingly, but honestly. On the other hand, *responding* to the truth must be done with humility and gentleness as well. If you laugh, attack, judge, or reject what is being said, you'll wound the one you love and endanger communication. Create a safe place for your future spouse to be heard, even when it's tough.

6. *Trust.* Marriage is the most intimate relationship on earth, and that makes you capable of being hurt. Always protect each other by concealing your intimate conversations and not exposing the other's wrongs or failures to outsiders.

Stan and Melanie found themselves in a crisis. Melanie saw some e-mails that Stan had sent to another woman—personal and intimate e-mails. Melanie confronted him, and although nothing physical went on between

Stan and the other woman, he repented and got counseling for his inappropriate behavior. Even in the midst of her feelings of hurt and betrayal, Melanie chose never to discuss Stan's behavior with anyone other than her counselor. Her choice to protect the privacy of her marriage allowed both of them to forgive, heal, and trust each other again.

What is private between you as a couple should remain private. Don't break the trust you have by discussing these matters with others, including your parents or siblings. The only other person who should be privy to personal details about your marriage would be a pastor or counselor. If the situation is one in which a spouse is in danger and doesn't have a pastor or

Ask the Expert

"What is your primary love language? What makes you feel most loved by your spouse? What do you desire above all else?" asks Gary Chapman.[1] Chapman's book *The Five Love Languages* shows you how to unselfishly show your future spouse love by sharing it in the way he or she can best receive it. It's expressed through his or her "love language." Which of the following love languages best communicates love to you and to your future spouse?

1. Words of affirmation
2. Quality time
3. Receiving gifts
4. Acts of service
5. Physical touch

How do you need to receive love? How does your future spouse need to receive love? If you learn to show love the way your future spouse needs to receive it, you'll be communicating lovingly and unselfishly.

counselor to turn to, he or she should confide in someone who he or she knows is trustworthy, or even contact the authorities for help.

7. Perseverance. There may be times when you are so frustrated that trying to communicate barely seems worth the effort. But hang in there. Perseverance has a way of overcoming and bringing success. Believe the best in your mate and in your relationship, even if you think you'll never be able to make the other person understand you. The struggles you may sometimes face in communicating don't have to threaten your relationship. A positive, hopeful attitude mixed with empathy, love, and openness can help your relationship grow strong, even when communication is tough.

The qualities we've just mentioned, such as patience and honesty, contribute to loving communication, but there are other factors as well. Recognizing the differences in communication styles early can save frustration later. And two other key components—body language and listening—must be considered when striving to have good communication skills. We'll look at these elements in the following sections.

Communication Styles

In the previous chapter, we talked about some of the differences in the way each gender thinks and processes information. Men and women often communicate differently in style, content, emotion, speed, and so on. Women tend to be open communicators, while men are often quiet thinkers. Men often find it harder to articulate thoughts and feelings than women. No wonder we need patience with each other! I [Susan] have seen women who try to force their husbands to talk. They push and prod or demean and nag them out of sheer frustration, but they still don't get the response they want.

Men have often been taught that showing their feelings is a sign of weakness. Women, on the other hand, can often be so emotional that they confuse men into silence. An Iowa State University study showed that most women have a better command of language, but sometimes they overpower and intimidate men, even manipulate them, with their communication skills.[2]

Before I [Susan] married, I sublet my home to 10 women over an 8-year period. Emotional communication? You bet! Try having 5 women share a home together, and you'll see all kinds of communication styles—from emotional to manipulative. The common denominator was this: all of us liked to talk.

There are, of course, exceptions to this generality. The point is, men and women need to find a balance, a middle ground that enables them to communicate effectively. That may mean both partners in a relationship have to stretch a little—or a lot!

Some spouses may have to leave the comfort zone of quiet contemplation and express painful emotions, such as fear. Other spouses may have to leave the comfort zone of saying anything they want, when they want, and be sensitive to their mates. I've had to learn patience in determining when to speak, where to speak, and how much to say not only in my relationship with my husband but also in my relationships with co-workers, friends, and family. It's part of the journey we all make toward mature and effective communication.

Most couples have to learn to strike a balance between factual communication (communicating basic facts and information) and emotional communication (communicating feelings) and how to relate to each other in love. It's an ongoing process to be sure, but as long as you're determined to communicate well, your relationship will benefit from the effort you put forth.

Body Language

It's not just your words that matter. It's the content, the tone of your voice, and the nonverbal signals you send. Your words, attitudes, and actions all work together to send a clear message.

For some people, though, communication is a difficult task. I [Susan] have a brother who has special needs and struggles to communicate. It takes a lot of patience to understand his heart and know what he's trying to say. But because I love him and value who he is as a person, I muster the patience to ask a lot of questions just to get one answer and sit in silence as he figures out how to say what he's thinking.

Loving your future mate enough to take the time and expend the energy to fully communicate with him or her is critical to the development and depth of any relationship. To have healthy communication, your behavior, your facial expressions, and the tone of your voice must match your words. "You're right" can mean you're mad, sad, happy, afraid, humble, or proud, depending on the way you say it, as well as your body language.

You probably understand this well from your days as a teenager; we all do. Mom or Dad would say, "Watch your tone of voice, young woman!" or "Change that attitude, young man!" Much of the maturing process depends on learning how your tone of voice and body language affect how others receive what you say. Some communication experts say that communication is 38 percent tone, 55 percent body language, and only 7 percent words![3]

Some of your body language may be confusing to your future spouse. Although your actions may be just unconscious habits, they can be misunderstood. Folding your arms can make you feel secure, but it can also be

Steps to Improving Your Conversations

Here are a few guidelines for improving communication with your future mate:

1. Start with topics that interest both of you.
2. Practice good listening skills.
3. Go deeper with facts and information about each other.
4. Engage intellectually and give your opinion on certain issues.
5. Get real by sharing your emotions and concerns.
6. Develop intimate communication by sharing your heart, speaking the truth, and being honest with each other.

interpreted as a closed attitude that says, "I don't care, and I'm not going to listen to you or even consider a change."

In fact, I [Susan] have been misunderstood in the past because I get cold easily and tend to fold my arms to stay warm. But folding my arms communicated disinterest or standoffishness when I was, in fact, very interested in the conversation. So I've had to learn to monitor my actions and make them align with my intentions.

Good communication involves conveying what's in your heart and knowing that your future spouse will lovingly receive it. When you express your thoughts and your future spouse listens and responds with understanding, you both become successful communicators.

Listening

The truth is, many of us have never really learned to listen well. During a conversation, most of us concentrate on what we plan to say next rather than listening to what the other person is saying. We've learned to be selective listeners, sifting information, ignoring details, and allowing ourselves to be distracted by everything around us. All day long I [Susan] sift information at work, so when I come home, I have to consciously shift gears to engage on a more intimate level with my husband.

To listen well, you have to be considerate of the other person's need to communicate with you. That means you have to choose to shut out the distractions around you and engage that person with your eyes, ears, and heart, giving him or her your undivided attention. Sometimes turning down the music or shutting off the television is important for good communication; at other times, you might need to take a walk to get away from distractions. Whatever setting you choose for a conversation, your objective is to find out what your future spouse is really trying to say.

Once you've heard what your future spouse has to say, you then need to verify that you understand what he or she meant. If you repeat back what you

Build Your Communication Skills

- Morning and evening chats. Start and end your day with a few minutes of uninterrupted conversation time.
- Home-from-work transition time to connect. When one or both of you get home from work, take a few minutes to reconnect. However, if one of you needs a few moments of personal time before you're ready to talk and share, understand and accept this about each other. Perhaps your spouse needs 15 minutes of quiet time before he or she is ready to talk about your days.
- Kiss 'n' hug. Don't go a day without giving each other a heartfelt kiss and hug. It may sound silly now, but later in your marriage, it'll be a tradition you'll be grateful you established.
- Mealtimes. Take time to pray together before meals, and use mealtimes as a time for conversation. Turn off the TV and make the effort to talk and connect during this time.
- Dates. Never lose the romance. Go on dates regularly, and guys, if she says she needs a date, listen to her! Remember that a date doesn't have to cost money. Be creative in finding ways to spend time together.
- Prayer time. Establish daily prayer time together. For us, it's morning, night, and mealtimes, and we even pray during news commercials!
- Decision time. When decisions need to be made or concerns need to be aired, set aside a specific time to do so.

heard your future mate say and then let him or her respond to what you said, that will help clarify whatever you may not have understood or what he or she may not have articulated well. Following these simple steps will help ensure that you and your future mate are communicating with understanding.

What About Me?

Read the following statements and evaluate how well you do in each area by checking the appropriate space:

	Usually	Sometimes	I Need Improvement
I patiently listen.	_____	_____	_____
I communicate with kindness.	_____	_____	_____
I avoid being envious.	_____	_____	_____
I resist prideful boasting.	_____	_____	_____
I refuse to speak rudely.	_____	_____	_____
I control my thought life.	_____	_____	_____
I communicate unselfishly.	_____	_____	_____
I rarely get angry.	_____	_____	_____
I easily forgive.	_____	_____	_____
I am truthful.	_____	_____	_____
I protect our private conversations.	_____	_____	_____
I trust our relationship.	_____	_____	_____
I hope for the best in our conversations.	_____	_____	_____
I persevere when we struggle to communicate.	_____	_____	_____
I am committed to improving our communication skills.	_____	_____	_____

Note: You may find this exercise as well as the following "What About Us?" exercise difficult to discuss with your future mate. If so, now is the time to rely on your pastor, a counselor, a mature couple, or your small group to help you work through these exercises.

What About Us?

Now evaluate your relationship as a couple in the following areas by reading each statement and checking the appropriate space:

	Usually	*Sometimes*	*We Need Improvement*
We patiently communicate.	____	____	____
We are kind to each other.	____	____	____
We don't envy each other.	____	____	____
Prideful boasting isn't part of our communication.	____	____	____
We aren't rude with each other.	____	____	____
Our conversations are unselfish.	____	____	____
We don't often get angry with each other.	____	____	____
We forgive each other.	____	____	____
We are truthful with each other.	____	____	____
We protect each other.	____	____	____
We trust each other.	____	____	____
We hope for the best.	____	____	____
We persevere through tough conversations.	____	____	____
We will work to improve our communication.	____	____	____

Just for Fun!

Take turns telling each other a personal adventure story. It can be a fun memory, a scary memory, or a crazy memory. Just have fun sharing with each other! (And take this opportunity to practice your listening skills.)

What Does God Say?

Loving communication is a scriptural mandate. Read the following scriptures and discuss how they relate to your communication. Then indicate which 1 Corinthians 13 principles (listed below) describe what the verse is talking about. (*Note:* There will be more than one principle for some of the verses.)

1 Corinthians 13 Principles

Patience	Faithfulness ("Love never fails")
Kindness	Trust
Truthfulness	Perseverance
Forgiveness	Humility
Protection	

Put away perversity from your mouth; keep corrupt talk far from your lips. (Proverbs 4:24)

Principle(s):

Reckless words pierce like a sword, but the tongue of the wise brings healing. (Proverbs 12:18)

Principle(s):

A wise man's heart guides his mouth, and his lips promote instruction. (Proverbs 16:23)

Principle(s):

He who covers over an offense promotes love, but whoever repeats the matter separates close friends. (Proverbs 17:9)

Principle(s):

A man of knowledge uses words with restraint, and a man of understanding is even-tempered. (Proverbs 17:27)

Principle(s):

Listen to advice and accept instruction, and in the end you will be wise. (Proverbs 19:20)

Principle(s):

He who guards his mouth and his tongue keeps himself from calamity. (Proverbs 21:23)

Principle(s):

Get rid of all bitterness, rage and anger, brawling and slander, along with every form of malice. Be kind and compassionate to one another, forgiving each other, just as in Christ God forgave you. (Ephesians 4:31–32)

Principle(s):

Do nothing out of selfish ambition or vain conceit, but in humility consider others better than yourselves. Each of you should look not only to your own interests, but also to the interests of others. (Philippians 2:3–4)

Principle(s):

Do not lie to each other, since you have taken off your old self with its practices and have put on the new self, which is being renewed in knowledge in the image of its Creator. (Colossians 3:9–10)

Principle(s):

Therefore, as God's chosen people, holy and dearly loved, clothe yourselves with compassion, kindness, humility, gentleness and patience. Bear with each other and forgive whatever grievances you may have against one another. Forgive as the Lord forgave you. And over all these virtues put on love, which binds them all together in perfect unity. (Colossians 3:12–14)

Principle(s):

Take note of this: Everyone should be quick to listen, slow to speak and slow to become angry. (James 1:19)

Principle(s):

7

Rules of Engagement

How Do You Fight Fair?

D ave was an all-American jock. While in high school, he broke a 17-year-old track record. He'd always been conscientious, maybe even an overachiever, but Dave worked hard to develop his skills and strengthen his game. The lessons Dave learned from competition, teamwork, and perseverance have a lot to do with his determination to resolve conflict in healthy ways.

As a young girl, Katie, now Dave's wife, missed most of those lessons and instead learned some unhealthy habits of dealing with problems. As a result, Katie and Dave struggled with how to resolve conflict during their first few months of marriage. Every time an argument or difficult situation arose, Katie tended to become defensive, was easily offended, and reacted with emotional outbursts. Eventually she realized how unhealthy her behavior was. She met with a counselor, read several self-help books, and worked with Dave to learn better patterns of resolving conflict. As they celebrated their first anniversary, Dave and Katie reflected on their progress and how learning to deal with conflict in positive ways had strengthened their relationship.

Whether in sports, careers, or personal relationships, conflicts will arise. In order to be successful in resolving them, you must learn the skill of healthy conflict resolution and then practice it until you're comfortable, confident, and capable. Many of us have learned to flee from conflict, make excuses, attack others, or become spectators rather than players.

This chapter will help you establish healthy ways to settle your disagreements so that neither you nor your future spouse will end up with emotional wounds or failures in your relationship. If you're like Katie and have learned

What's Your MO (Mode of Operation)?

Reflecting on how you naturally tend to handle disagreements will help you understand what conflict-resolution pattern you may have formed. What do you and your future mate instinctively tend to do when you disagree? Try these scenarios on for size—and be honest:

1. Your future husband makes plans to go out with his friends, even though you already had plans to go out together. How would you most likely respond?

    A. Yell at him or sarcastically tell him how inconsiderate and unloving he is.

    B. Pout about it and hope he'll figure out what he did wrong.

    C. Hesitate about sharing your feelings, stuff them, and fret.

    D. Explain how it feels unloving and disrespectful when he breaks his commitments.

2. When buying wedding favors for your big day, your future wife exceeds the budget you agreed on by hundreds of dollars. How would you typically respond?

    A. Get angry and tell her how irresponsible she is.

unhealthy conflict-resolution patterns in the past, this chapter will help you recognize those patterns and establish healthier habits.

CONFLICTING ATTITUDES

There are usually four different attitudes people have toward conflict:
- I'll win! (You control or attack and see your mate as the enemy.)

(continued)

        B. Give her the silent treatment and stew about it.

        C. Walk away from the discussion, rationalizing that it's her problem.

        D. Discuss the consequences of spending money that's unbudgeted and figure out how you both can have some regular spending money.

3. As a bride-to-be, you listen to your future mother-in-law complain about your wedding plans. How would you likely respond?

        A. Get angry at her interference and tell your future husband to set her straight.

        B. Don't say anything because you don't want to cause friction before the wedding.

        C. Ignore her, but complain about her to your mother.

        D. Discuss the options and respectfully tell her that you and her son are making the final plans.

If you tended toward the A answers, you may have an assertive "I'll win!" MO; if you tended toward the Bs, you may have a passive "I'll never win" MO; if the Cs, you may be an avoider; and if the Ds, you may want to compromise and settle things together.

- I'll never win. (You give up before even trying to resolve issues.)
- I'll withdraw. (You think, *I'll just let it go.*)
- We'll work together and find a way to resolve the issue.

What's your attitude? Most of us hate confrontation and would rather avoid it than take risks to resolve a problem. When you're dating, you usually try to push your differences aside to create peace and harmony. But eventually you'll agitate your future spouse or rub him or her the wrong way. Then you'll have to decide how to solve your disagreements.

Commitment to the relationship must be the foundation on which you choose to resolve conflict. In fact, from the very beginning of your marriage, vow *never* to use the D word (divorce). Threatening divorce implies that you're not truly committed to the relationship and that you could choose to leave your spouse when things get rough.

The truth is, God wants to use all things for His and your good. Romans 8:28 says, "We know that in all things God works for the good of those who love him, who have been called according to his purpose." So you should ask: What can I learn from this conflict? How can this help us grow as a couple?

DEVELOP A PLAN

One of your primary marriage goals should be to establish a healthy pattern of resolving differences right from the start. It's better to realize now that you may have some poor skills and work to establish good patterns rather than take those unhealthy patterns into your marriage and hurt your spouse.

Perhaps your father used anger as a way of controlling, or your mother selfishly manipulated your dad to get what she wanted. Maybe there was shouting or name-calling, or perhaps sarcasm was used to end a disagreement. Or maybe silence controlled the atmosphere of your home when your parents got into a spat.

Begin now to assess what you learned from your family. Commit to leave the poor patterns behind, and replace them with healthy ways to resolve conflict. It took me [Susan] years to leave old patterns behind and figure out how to resolve conflict in a healthy way. Don't let it take years for you.

Equip yourself with the skills of conflict resolution and accommodate each other's exhaustion, apprehension, or emotions. It has to be a joint effort, and winning as a team should be the focus. It takes time, patience, and skill to learn how to do it well, but it's worth it, and now is the time to learn and grow.

Maybe you haven't yet had a disagreement. One thing's for sure: you will! To deny this reality is asking for trouble. When a couple never disagrees or has differing opinions, ideas, or values, they usually have a relationship in which one partner is willing to compromise at any cost. But in a healthy relationship, you should both feel you can safely communicate what you think, believe, feel, and need.

To make settling every conflict a win-win situation for both of you, strive to understand the heart of the person you fell in love with, and make his or her needs and feelings your top priority—ahead of any disagreement. We're not saying that you'll never win or be right in a disagreement, but resolving conflict together to the satisfaction of each of you is the right approach. Then you'll see how quickly all kinds of issues, big and small, can easily be resolved.

Round One: What to Expect

Early in our marriage, Dale and I [Susan] disagreed about our TV-viewing habits. Choosing what I watch has to line up with Philippians 4:8, which tells us to think—and view, in my opinion—things that are pure, noble, and right. Dale just surfed channels to find whatever looked interesting. So we had multiple discussions about what we should let enter our hearts and minds through the media, and sometimes we didn't agree on what was appropriate. After we struggled through several disagreements, we finally came to a common ground that works for both of us.

Most of the time, if we both feel it's not a good show, we'll simply change the channel or turn off the TV. On rare occasions, when I'd rather not watch the movie or TV program, I'll find something else to do, such as read a book. But we've both learned to compromise in this area. There have been times when Dale has sat through a chick flick that I know he's not thrilled about. Now, even though we seldom sit down to an evening of TV viewing, when we do, we rarely disagree, and our evenings together are enjoyable.

The fact is that conflict can happen for many reasons: when your self-esteem is threatened, if you feel mistreated or misunderstood, if you feel you've been treated unjustly or unfairly, or even if one of you is just in a bad mood. Conflict may also arise when you've been criticized, when you've been expected to do too much, or when you've felt rejected.

Unrealized expectations and unmet needs—whether physical, emotional,

Ask the Experts

In their book *Safe Haven Marriage*, Dr. Archibald Hart and Dr. Sharon Hart Morris write,

> Can you envision a marriage in which you would feel safe enough to say what you feel? In which you are assured that your spouse would respect, or at least attempt to understand your point of view? Under those circumstances, at the end of an argument you could come back together and reestablish your emotional warmth. You would be able to say to each other, "I don't want to hurt you, and you don't want to hurt me."[1]

Do you want to create a marriage based on solid trust? *Safe Haven Marriage* will help you learn valuable ways of communicating that will promote emotional closeness and understanding in your relationship.

intellectual, spiritual, or financial—cause many conflicts. Issues of safety, values, roles, attitudes, friends, honesty, trust, or any number of other things can also trigger disagreements.

We all know that we come into a relationship with flaws and weaknesses that can cause conflict, whether it's an annoying habit, an inconsiderate behavior, thoughtless words, or offensive actions. The reality is that the closer you are to someone, the more you risk being hurt. You know each other's tender spots. You know what hot buttons to push.

For some people, a sensitive spot might be feeling disrespected, ignored, or unappreciated; for others, it could be feeling unloved or unsafe. If either partner touches a sensitive area, there's bound to be conflict.

So what can you do? Whether it's a little spat over a minor difference of opinion or a heated argument or a debate over an important subject, such as finances or sex, a disagreement should never escalate into a hostile fight that causes either partner to feel afraid, rejected, or alienated. You can win a fight and lose valuable territory in the areas of trust and respect, or you can embrace the opportunity to find greater intimacy by dealing with the inevitable conflicts that may arise.

Resolving conflict can be a scary thing, but if you fear the process, you'll often leave a problem unresolved. Choosing to deal with issues will keep problems small and help you work toward a healthy relationship.

ROUND TWO: RECOGNIZING THE SOURCE

Some issues can be a constant source of friction in marriage—money, sex, children, in-laws, work, time together, and more. When you find yourselves arguing about the same things over and over again, a couple of issues may be at play: one or both of you may be demonstrating stubbornness, a refusal to bend and compromise, or there may be a deeper issue, such as a clash of values.

In the first case, stubbornness won't ever help solve disagreements, so if you're the one digging in your heels when you fight about the same thing over and over, step back and ask yourself why. You may simply need to be more flexible, or you may need to change your attitude.

If you think the cause of your arguments is a clash of values, it's best to discuss things in light of God's Word. Does Scripture have something to say about what you're arguing about? Is the issue contrary to God's view of the situation? If so, settle things according to what the Bible says. If neither of these scenarios applies, and you still can't resolve a recurring argument, it might be helpful to discuss the situation with an older couple you respect, your pastor, or a counselor to get an objective view of the deeper issue.

ROUND THREE: FIGHTING FAIR

Resolving conflict isn't effective when one of you feels that you must win every disagreement, no matter what. Yet that's what many people do; they attack their spouses and criticize or blame them, breaking trust or hurting them so badly that they cringe at the thought of any future confrontation. All their partners want to do is avoid being hurt again.

Some people do all the compromising, leaving their partners to claim ultimate victory while they become afraid and bitter. For others, repressing or stuffing conflict brings resentment. Some even spiritualize the problem, saying that God will take care of it, so they can avoid doing anything about it. Simply put, if you choose not to do the work it takes to resolve disagreements with your future spouse, you won't achieve the true intimacy your heart seeks.

STEPS TO RESOLVING CONFLICT

Let's get practical. The object of conflict resolution is to exchange information, understand each other, and come to a solution that works for both of you without wounding each other. Because intimacy is built on freedom, honesty, and safety, allow each other to freely, honestly, and safely discuss any problems that may arise.

The following 10 A's of successful conflict resolution will help equip you to constructively resolve personal conflicts with your future mate:

1. Attitude: prepare your heart. Make your relationship the top priority, not your personal differences or opinions.

Anger is a normal emotion when a person is hurt, frustrated, afraid, or confused. Everyone gets upset, but when you don't control your responses, you'll hurt your relationship. When you're frustrated, try to understand what you're feeling, and take control of your thoughts and emotions before speaking or responding poorly.

If you're on the receiving end of a negative outburst, what can you do to calm a heated situation, bring your future mate security, and defuse anger? First, realize you can only control *your* thoughts, emotions, and actions; you can't control your loved one's. You have to choose not to react in anger, even if your spouse has already reacted badly.

Your future mate may also send you signals that communicate you've hurt him or her. Signals may include becoming silent, walking away, avoiding the situation, or changing the subject. Watch for these clues and learn what signals your partner typically sends when he or she is hurt or upset. If you see that you've hurt your future mate, ask about it. Don't expect to read each other's minds.

Accept the fact that none of us is perfect; everyone makes mistakes—even you. Realize, too, that we rarely mean to intentionally hurt the one we love. Unless you're marrying a mean-spirited or abusive person (which we advise you not to do), your future mate will usually have good intentions. So give grace to him or her in the situation.

Especially during conflict, both of you should practice the listening skills you learned in the previous chapter. Good listening habits create security and openness in a relationship. You show how deeply you care by accepting your partner for who he or she is and accepting what your future spouse feels.

Choose not to react too quickly; avoid overreacting, being too emotional, or becoming overly dramatic; and try to see the other person's viewpoint.

2. Ask: let God guide you. It's not always easy, but Susan and I [Dale] pray together before we work through a conflict. It calms us down, realigns our thinking, and unites our spirits. And it humbles us. Though this might not always work in the heat of the moment, when you both approach a problem in an honest, sincere, and humble way, and you request the Lord's help in solving the problem, the outcome will often surprise you.

When you face differing opinions on serious subjects as a couple, you'll be able to more easily resolve the problem as you turn to prayer and the Bible to see what God would have you do. Your faith will be challenged, but in the process, you'll grow closer as a couple.

3. Assume: take ownership of your emotions. Assume responsibility for your own emotions. Never let your feelings or words escalate into hurtful situations. If you got angry and yelled at your future wife when she did something wrong, take responsibility for losing your temper and apologize. If you got upset at your future mate and you gave him the silent treatment for working late and missing your date night, apologize for your manipulative behavior.

Try to control your reactions, both verbal and nonverbal. Avoid blaming, accusing, belittling, name-calling, yelling, or monopolizing the discussion. Owning your emotions also means that you don't walk away from an argument; instead, work through it respectfully.

Resolving conflict takes a lot of self-control. Under the stress of a disagreement, your perspective often gets distorted. When this happens, stop, take some time out or a few deep breaths, calm yourself, and then go back to resolving the situation. Many couples we've counseled have learned to take time out before attempting to resolve a conflict. It helps them regroup before returning to the discussion.

Remember that trust, safety, and security go a long way in bringing about successful conflict resolution. Trust means giving each other the benefit of the doubt and realizing that there may be other things that triggered the anger or conflict. Give each other space to work through conflict without being judged or rejected.

4. Analyze: define the real problem. This isn't the time for silence or with-drawing. Attack the problem, not the person. It's not your responsibility to change your partner; your objective is to help him or her see the problem through your eyes and understand why you think there needs to be a change.

Again, this takes a lot of self-control. Ephesians 4:26 says, "In your anger do not sin." Step back, analyze the problem, write down your thoughts, and prepare for a positive discussion. It will keep you on track and help you express all your thoughts in a constructive way.

What's beneath the surface of your irritation or offense? Sometimes either Susan or I [Dale] will become moody because we're frustrated about something at the office or an issue with our adult children, only to discover that the irritation we're placing on the other has nothing to do with him or her.

Take time to consider the underlying problem. Is it an annoying behavior? An unbiblical attitude? Unmet expectations? A need? An offense? A fear? An unmet desire? A clash of values? Why is this issue such a big deal to you? Whatever the problem is, try to verbalize it in one sentence; tell your future mate precisely what is troubling you. For example: "I feel disrespected when you tell your friends about mistakes I've made" or "I feel unloved when you make plans with your friends without discussing it with me first."

Could something in your past be triggering your feelings? Sometimes the way your parents lost their tempers might trigger fear or a feeling of rejection when you see something similar in your future mate. Be sure both of you understand the real issue. Give a clear, direct, concise statement of the problem, without accusation or blame. Be honest and personal.

5. Atmosphere: provide the right time and place. Providing the right time and place to work through a conflict will offer both of you the best possibility of resolving the issue. If one of you is a morning person and the other prefers to stay up late, meeting sometime during the day would probably be best.

Never argue in public. If you do get into a disagreement in public, step aside and agree together to settle it later. Better yet, develop a sign or a signal between the two of you, such as mouthing the word *later* (or something like this) to alert the other that you'd rather finish the discussion in private.

Resolving issues should become a top priority—above your busy schedules, plans with friends, or your favorite TV show. On one occasion, Dale and I [Susan] canceled a get-together and let the answering machine take phone calls—and we're glad we did. We needed several uninterrupted hours to talk through things. Resolving a problem shouldn't be a spur-of-the-moment, off-the-cuff explosion.

If at all possible, try to settle the problem before the day's end. At the same time, don't try to force a conversation if you are tired, are emotional, or have distractions (such as company or children) that will impede a productive discussion. You might have to agree to settle things in the morning.

Take time to organize your thoughts; choose a quiet, comfortable place free from distractions (TV, computer, kids, etc.), and give yourself enough time to work through the issue. But don't continue a discussion to the point of exhaustion. Sometimes you may have to table the discussion until you're rested. One disagreement Dale and I had took two days to resolve. We talked about it, had to table it and move on with our days, and then return to settle it after we had time to think about it.

6. *Articulate: speak the truth in love.* You're finally ready to discuss the problem. Here are a few tips to help you do that:

- Use "I" statements instead of "you" statements when you talk about the problem. Say "I feel unappreciated when you don't thank me for dinner," not "You never appreciate all the work I do to make meals!"
- Avoid using explosive words, pushing hot buttons, or launching verbal attacks. Try not to allow an irritable edge in your voice and body language that confronts rather than connects. Be careful not to shout, use sarcasm, or speak in a condescending tone. Don't interrupt or revisit old conflicts. Stick to the subject at hand. If you can't talk without doing this, you need more time to collect yourself.

- Be careful to monitor the volume of your voice. Speak directly and make your thoughts known in a loving way. Take responsibility for your own part of the problem.
- Present your viewpoint, but then listen carefully to your future mate's point of view. Give each other the same time and opportunity to provide feedback.

7. Assess: listen with your heart and respond with love. Listening to your future spouse in the midst of an argument may be the toughest yet most important thing you can do. Listen with your heart, eyes, and body. When you listen with your heart, you keep your attitude in check.

When your future mate can't clearly express a concern, be patient. Ask questions and give him or her time to explain. Try to understand your loved one's point of view as you remember that he or she loves you and isn't trying to hurt you.

Respectfully give immediate feedback regarding what you heard your future spouse say. Restate what you thought you heard, because people often misunderstand or misinterpret what was actually said.

8. Agree: find a solution together. In seeking a solution, don't demand or jump to a specific solution from the start. Conflict resolution is a discovery process, and it may take some time to find the answer that's right for both of you.

Be open-minded and explore the options. Discuss what each of you can do to help solve the problem. Focus on options that have the best chance of ensuring a win-win situation, and eliminate all the possibilities that will only add fuel to the fire.

Resistance to change and compromise is normal, but understand that each of you will likely have to compromise a little, or sometimes a lot, to reach a solution. But when you do compromise, your loved one will recognize your honest effort to make things better, and this can strengthen your relationship even more than the actual solution.

Complex issues such as budgeting, vocational choices, or major lifestyle changes may need to be studied carefully before any solution can be reached. Not all problems can be solved in one discussion. Realize that you may need professional help in some situations. That's not only okay, but it may be imperative at times. Maybe you need a counselor to help you work through your anger issues. Perhaps you need to sit down with a financial planner to establish a healthy budget.

Sometimes there are areas where you just have to agree to disagree. That's okay too. If it's not an area of moral wrong but is just an area of preference or an opinion, then let it go by not revisiting it. When you finally do agree on a solution, support that mutual decision together.

9. Answer: forgive and resolve. Recognize that one or both of you must often experience a change of heart to fully resolve a problem. If it's you, be humble enough to admit it, ask for forgiveness, and choose to change. If it's your future spouse, forgive him or her wholeheartedly. Don't demand an apology. You have to choose to let go of the pain that the conflict brought. Don't deny your hurt; acknowledge it and then forgive.

Forgiveness will help you move on and keep the past from interfering with your relationship. It restores trust and safety, brings confidence back into the relationship, and yields greater intimacy and peace.

Remember, just as God forgave you, so you should forgive others (Colossians 3:13). Forgiveness is a choice to let go of what happened and rekindle your love so you can grow in your relationship.

How can you do that? Pray together, forgive each other, and trust God to help you heal and move on. Then affirm your love and support for one another. Thank each other for the honesty and hard work you both put into arriving at an agreement.

What if your future spouse stubbornly refuses to arrive at a solution? Let God deal with him or her. You aren't the Holy Spirit. Love and pray for your future spouse and let the Lord work within your partner as only He can. But remember, if there's abuse or neglect in your relationship, get help from a professional counselor, your family, the church, or the authorities.

10. Applaud: celebrate a job well done. Finally, when you've resolved a conflict, reward yourselves with something you both enjoy. It could be a night out, a walk in the park, or just a bowl of ice cream by candlelight—anything that says, "Together, we did a good job!"

Resolving conflict requires a positive attitude, good communication skills, and a humble heart. As you continually work at solving your problems together, you'll successfully solve your disagreements, and your relationship will grow stronger through it.

What About Me?

How did your parents handle conflict? Did they avoid it, fight unfairly, or work together to resolve things? Discuss this with your future mate.

When you have conflicts with your future mate, do you tend to control, attack, blame, withdraw, ignore, give up, or work to resolve the problem?

What areas do you need to work on to improve your way of resolving conflicts?

What About Us?

Review what has caused some of the conflicts between the two of you. Did they come about because of misunderstandings? Unrealized expectations? Unmet needs? Annoying habits? Be careful as you talk about each conflict, and discuss the underlying causes. Don't argue about how your fiancé(e) feels or the way he or she responds. Focus on understanding him or her.

Just for Fun!

Who would you say is your role model (other than God or your parents)? Why?

Which of the five senses is most important to you and why?

What Does God Say?

If we believe the Bible is the owner's manual for our lives, then it has wisdom for every problem we face. Following God's Word and knowing His character is always the best way to resolve conflict.

In summary, here's what God's Word says about the 10 A's of successful conflict resolution:

1. *Attitude: prepare your heart.* Ephesians 4:31–32 says, "Get rid of all bitterness, rage and anger, brawling and slander, along with every

form of malice. Be kind and compassionate to one another, forgiving each other, just as in Christ God forgave you."

2. *Ask: let God guide you.* James 3:17–18 says, "The wisdom that comes from heaven is first of all pure; then peace-loving, considerate, submissive, full of mercy and good fruit, impartial and sincere. Peacemakers who sow in peace raise a harvest of righteousness."

3. *Assume: take ownership of your emotions.* Proverbs 28:13 says, "He who conceals his sins does not prosper, but whoever confesses and renounces them finds mercy."

4. *Analyze: define the real problem.* James 4:1 says, "What causes fights and quarrels among you? Don't they come from your desires that battle within you?"

5. *Atmosphere: provide the right time and place.* First Peter 4:8 says, "Above all, love each other deeply, because love covers over a multitude of sins."

6. *Articulate: speak the truth in love.* Ephesians 4:15 says, "Instead, speaking the truth in love, we will in all things grow up into him who is the Head, that is, Christ."

7. *Assess: listen with your heart and respond with love.* Proverbs 12:15 says, "The way of a fool seems right to him, but a wise man listens to advice."

8. *Agree: find a solution together.* Proverbs 20:3 says, "It is to a man's honor to avoid strife, but every fool is quick to quarrel."

9. *Answer: forgive and resolve.* Colossians 3:12–15 says, "Therefore, as God's chosen people, holy and dearly loved, clothe yourselves with compassion, kindness, humility, gentleness and patience. Bear with each other and forgive whatever grievances you may have against one another. Forgive as the Lord forgave you. And over all these virtues put on love, which binds them all together in perfect unity."

10. *Applaud: celebrate a job well done.* Philippians 4:8 says, "Finally, brothers, whatever is true, whatever is noble, whatever is right, whatever is pure, whatever is lovely, whatever is admirable—if anything is excellent or praiseworthy—think about such things."

8

LET'S MAKE CENTS

How Do You Navigate Your Financial Life?

Jack wasn't used to doing without. His parents had provided all he ever wanted or needed, and he'd never had to budget for anything. The financial struggles he and his wife, Monica, continually faced weren't what he'd bargained for. He'd expected that their two-income marriage would provide greater freedom to buy the things he wanted.

Monica, on the other hand, was used to scrimping, saving, and setting financial goals. After all, she came from a single-parent home where they all had to watch every penny, and she even had to plan months ahead to afford her prom dress. Budgeting, planning, and saving were a frame of reference and a safe place for Monica.

But now, Monica and Jack were frustrated. After trying to make a family budget work for more than three years, every month they fell short. More and more debt accumulated until they feared bankruptcy might be their only option.

Jack's online spending habits were out of control, especially when it came to bidding on eBay. His unbudgeted purchases caused so much conflict, stress, and debt that eventually his choices threatened their marriage. Something had to change.

WHAT'S YOUR FINANCIAL HISTORY?

All of us grow up with attitudes about money. Most of us acquired our view of money from our parents, while others may have been influenced by close friends or even the culture. Whether our parents were wealthy, poor, or in between, we're in some way influenced by that history.

I [Dale] grew up in a family that practiced good financial habits. Yet a catastrophic illness and the subsequent death of my older brother broke our family financially. Two years later, my father died of a heart attack when I was just 13.

Fortunately, I had already learned the essentials of good money management from my dad. I learned that you must be willing to work hard, have goals, be honest, not spend more than you make, save at least 10 percent of what you make, stay out of debt, and let your money work for you by making wise investments (with professional help, if needed). I also learned not to gamble or take unnecessary risks. Thanks to my dad, I realized that managing money well really wasn't that complicated. And because of my experiences growing up, I gained an appreciation of financial security and an understanding of the importance of self-discipline and careful living.

My [Susan's] parents, however, didn't talk about financial matters, so I grew up with little understanding about how to manage money. When I became an adult, I was unsure and fearful of taking on the responsibility of money management, and it took me many painful years to gain the skills needed to handle money well.

Whether you've made wise financial decisions up to this point or more bad choices than good, if you'll both take to heart the financial principles that we'll lay out in this chapter, you can begin your marriage with a clear, united perspective of how you'll handle your finances together.

First, think back to how you grew up. How did your parents handle money? What was your family's attitude regarding finances? Answer the following questions honestly, understanding that your past financial experiences can affect your marriage positively or negatively.

- Did you grow up rich, poor, or middle class?
- What value did you learn to place on money?
- Were you secure or insecure about money?
- Did your parents model generosity, good shopping habits, and careful planning?
- Was work more important than family? Was pleasure more important than wise money management?
- Did your parents use coupons, pay bills on time, and meet financial goals?
- Was there gambling, overspending, or a keeping-up-with-the-Joneses mentality?
- Did either of your parents engage in high-risk deals or get-rich-quick schemes?
- Did your parents have the idea that bankruptcy is okay?
- Did your family sacrifice when needed, save, invest, and work on a cash basis?
- Were insurance, health care, and retirement important to your parents?
- Did they live on the edge of their finances to enjoy life now and not worry about tomorrow?

Now that you've talked about the past, let's talk a little about the present. Consider your current financial status. (We'll look at this deeper in the "What About Me?" section at the end of the chapter.)

Can you see obvious areas of your life in which your family's attitude regarding money has influenced your financial choices? If so, discuss this with your future mate.

Do you have friends who are rich, and does peer pressure sometimes push you to live beyond your means? Are you overly influenced by the culture and the media so that you think you need more than you can afford?

Your attitudes about money directly or indirectly influence the way you think and the decisions you make, so assessing whether you've had positive or negative financial influences in your life is imperative if you're to maintain a healthy view of money and finances.

FINANCIAL DANGER SIGNS

If either of you already has insufficient income to pay your bills, refuses to balance your checkbook regularly, has a get-rich-quick attitude (such as hoping to win the lottery), or is unwilling to work hard to make ends meet, these behaviors are signs of unhealthy financial thinking. A habit of borrowing, making purchases on credit, impulse buying, and paying only the minimum payment on a revolving credit account are also indicators of bad financial management. Other unhealthy attitudes and/or habits include making excuses, such as "I just don't understand money," "Why should I try?" or "What's money for if we can't spend it?"

Some people believe their situation is unique, and they use this excuse to justify financial indulgence. Others live beyond their means to present an image of success. These are all warning signs of poor stewardship, a lack of maturity, or a lack of financial common sense. It's best to work through these problems now. An irresponsible financial attitude will certainly affect you and hurt your relationship with your future mate.

WHAT DOES IT MATTER?

Money causes more problems in marriage than most of us realize. Before you marry, you're often trying to impress your future mate, so you may not want to mess things up by discussing finances. You may think, *I'll cross that bridge when I get there.* But refusing to talk about something as important as financial management before you get married can be more costly than you might imagine.

Peter and Ellen didn't think about discussing finances before they married, but after they married, Ellen was shocked to find out that Peter had nearly fifty thousand dollars in school loans! In order to pay off the loans, these newlyweds moved in with Peter's parents. They lived in the basement and spent the first two years of their marriage putting both of their salaries into eliminating their debt. It was a hard beginning, but looking back, they're so glad they did what they had to do to pay off Peter's debt. Still, Peter and

Ask the Experts

Bethany and Scott Palmer's book *Cents and Sensibility* contains many helpful hints on how to resolve money issues. After you marry, you may want to dig deeper into sensible and responsible money management. But right now, here are a few questions the Palmers suggest you discuss with each other:

1. Do you think joint or separate checking accounts are appropriate in your marriage?
2. Do you think paying the bills should be done separately or together?
3. Do you work with a budget now?
4. Are you conservative or aggressive in your investing?
5. What are your income goals?
6. Have you ever lost a large amount of money?
7. What mistakes have you made with money?
8. What is the most expensive item you have ever purchased?
9. What stresses you out when it comes to money?
10. Do you track your saving and spending?
11. How important is planning for retirement to you?
12. Do you tithe and/or give to charitable organizations?[1]

Ellen agree that they should have taken the time to talk frankly about the financial aspect of their relationship before they married.

The truth is that money can bring a certain amount of happiness, but it can also be one of the biggest sources of stress in a marriage. You should both understand each other's spending and saving attitudes and habits.

Different Dynamics

There are a wide range of spending and saving habits, and although you can be different yet compatible, it's wise to know just how different you are when it comes to financial matters. The extremes can create a very stressful marriage.

The saver says, "A penny saved is a penny earned," while the spender thinks it's okay to "shop till you drop." The reality is that we have endless opportunities to buy, do, and go. That's the upside of our culture. But there's a serious downside too.

If one of you wants to save every penny while the other wants the latest brand-name fashions, enjoys eating out a lot, or loves to shop online even when you haven't budgeted for it, there's bound to be trouble.

The truth is, we spend more easily on things we value. Andrea and Corey discussed this early in their marriage. Corey liked buying tools and gadgets, so they added a budget item for this. Andrea liked eating out, so that became another important budget item. Assess what you enjoy and plan accordingly. Spenders and savers must honestly communicate their views on money and settle on a plan together to keep a balanced budget. And as a couple, you'll need to come to a mutual agreement on how much you'll spend and save, what sacrifices you'll make, and what priorities you'll establish.

We recently counseled an engaged couple, and when the topic of the young man's high truck payments came up, there was a lot of emotion in the negotiations. He loved his truck, but after a reality check, he realized he had to give it up to make ends meet. This wasn't an easy decision, but as the couple worked through the problem as a team, they found that they could indeed have diversity in their spending and saving habits and still live happily together. The negotiation required understanding and compromise on both sides.

Understanding money priorities and views can defuse conflicts, but that's only half the battle. Self-discipline and restraint are also critical components.

Together, answer the following questions regarding your current financial status and how you intend to handle financial management in the future.

- How do you feel about your financial situation right now? Are you comfortable, challenged, or overly stressed about your finances?
- How much will each of you earn?
- How much will each of you plan to save, and for what?
- How much will each of you be free to spend, and on what?
- How much are you willing to go into debt, and for what?
- Who will maintain the budget, pay the bills, and balance the checkbook?

Money Myths

Which of the following statements do you agree with?
- Money will make me content.
- Money will give me security.
- Money will bring me happiness.
- Money will make me popular.
- Money will give me freedom.
- You don't need to pay off credit cards each month.
- Borrowing money from family and friends is a good idea.

If you think any of these statements are true, beware! Each one is false and can cause financial problems down the road.

God ordained that we should become good stewards and manage our resources well. He wants us to acquire money honestly, invest it carefully, spend it wisely, and share it joyfully.

THE DEMON OF DEBT

Let's discuss a four-letter word that can really hurt a relationship: *debt.*

What is debt? It's everything you owe. It could be your mortgage, your car payment, student loans, credit-card balances, and so on. In our consumer culture, our list of perceived "must haves" just keeps growing, and we're willing to pay for these items, even if we must buy them on credit.

Matt and Colleen had a beautiful and extravagant wedding and an expensive honeymoon. Unfortunately, they went deep in debt for it—over and above the forty thousand dollars their parents gave them! But that was just the beginning of their financial woes.

Though they made a good income in New York, Matt lacked steady employment because he was in a commission-only industry, and although Colleen had a high-paying job, using credit cards became a way of life for them.

Eventually, Matt and Colleen found themselves well over fifty thousand dollars in debt. But they made only minimum monthly payments on their credit cards, paid high interest rates, and kept going deeper into debt. They even borrowed from family and friends. As they continued to spiral downward and increase debt, their only option seemed to be to claim bankruptcy. Meanwhile, their unhealthy financial management and poor choices caused extreme stress in their marriage.

So what's the lesson here? Matt and Colleen needed to learn to live within their means.

Some statistics say that 43 percent of families spend more than they make.[2] That means they're in debt, and debt is financial bondage! Romans 13:8 tells us, "Let no debt remain outstanding."

Dr. James Dobson, best-selling author and founder of Focus on the Family, put it well:

> Since we have limited resources and unlimited choices, the only
> way to get ahead financially is to deny ourselves some of the things
> we want. If we don't have the discipline to do that, then we will
> always be in debt.[3]

STINKIN' THINKIN'

Before you can balance your budget, you have to change the way you think about money and decide for yourself what's really important.

The pathway to financial freedom is one of discipline and proactive planning. If you're in debt, the first step to becoming successful financially is to admit you have a debt problem and to evaluate how you got into that situation. To do otherwise means you're in denial.

Find the courage and willingness to make things right with the businesses, friends, and family you owe money to, and then deal with the problem instead of ignoring or denying it. Owning your unhealthy attitude and habits and then proactively choosing to change are two good ways to begin your journey toward overcoming your debt.

Turn to God and ask Him for forgiveness, strength, courage, and wisdom to change your attitudes and behavior. Also, you and your future mate should forgive each other for past mistakes and discuss the changes that need to be made in order to begin your marriage with a determination to make wise financial choices.

The Bible says that "the love of money is a root of all kinds of evil" (1 Timothy 6:10). Understand that money itself isn't evil, but loving it often causes us to become controlled by it. We'll look at other biblical guidelines for managing money in the "What Does God Say?" section at the end of the chapter. Once we understand what God says in His Word—"The world is mine, and all that is in it" (Psalm 50:12)—we realize we're just stewards of what really belongs to Him.

STARTING OUT ON YOUR OWN

One of the biggest issues newlyweds often face is whether to ask family members for financial assistance. Young couples often face great financial challenges. They're beginning careers and have few material things, and they often bring school debt (and sometimes other debt) into the marriage. They may have received financial assistance for their wedding, but because there's so much pressure in today's society to have it all, they may be tempted to seek more financial assistance to get established quickly.

Once you marry, you should try to avoid getting your parents involved in your finances. There are other ways you can receive help from your parents without becoming dependent on their financial resources. Maybe you respect the advice they may provide. The Bible reminds us that it's not good to be indebted to anyone—and that includes parents (Proverbs 22:7). That's good advice, especially where family is involved.

There are often hidden risks that come with borrowing money from family or friends. Sometimes the borrower is embarrassed to ask for a loan, and the lender is put in an awkward position, even if he or she wants to help. Promises are made and both parties expect to honor the arrangement, but too often the situation changes and the debt is left unpaid. When this happens, the borrower feels guilty and ashamed, while the lender feels disappointed and even angry and resentful. And the relationship is damaged because expectations are left unfulfilled and trust gets broken. So we encourage you to avoid borrowing from others, and if a family member or friend does offer you money, it works best if it's a gift, not a loan. Relationships are simply too important to allow money to come between them.

When it's necessary to accept temporary assistance (from parents or other sources), make certain that the boundaries and expectations are clearly understood and established from the start, possibly even in writing. Everyone involved should be comfortable with the arrangement, whether you're accepting a gift or a loan, and in agreement about the terms.

Our friends Becky and Thom decided early in their marriage never to ask for financial help from their parents. They understood that this meant they would need to learn to live within their means, even sacrificing when necessary. At times this also meant not sharing their financial struggles with their parents because their parents tended to want to help them. After setting this financial boundary, they never expected or asked for financial assistance from them. Still, they gratefully accept the occasional financial gift, because they know their parents enjoy blessing them from time to time.

Pam and Ben struggled to get on their feet financially when they were newly married. So Ben's dad offered to build their dream home if they put an apartment in the basement for him. After the house was built and Ben's dad had moved in with them, they found that living with him was easier said than done. Disagreements, different values, and relational issues opened Pam and Ben's daily lives to critique, and they felt they didn't have the right to refuse his counsel. Eventually they sold their dream house and moved into a house they could afford without the assistance or input of Ben's father. After they freed themselves from the purse strings that made them feel obligated, they realized that they should have avoided financial ties to family from the start.

To set such boundaries, you and your future spouse should take the lead with your respective parents. Establishing clear boundaries when necessary will benefit you, your mate, and your parents.

CHOOSING TO CHANGE

Remember Jack and Monica from the beginning of the chapter? After debt nearly destroyed their marriage, they finally decided not only to change their thinking about money but also to change their lifestyle. They had to agree on what made good sense, they had to understand their spending habits and choose to make the necessary changes, and they had to work as a team as well as be accountable for creating and living within a budget. After a long, hard road back to financial stability, Jack and Monica's marriage became strong and peaceful as they learned to live responsibly together in love and trust.

Once you've changed your thinking, how do you become good stewards of what God has given you, and how do you blend both the finances and attitudes you bring into your marriage? Here's how to start:

1. *List all your income, expenses, and debt individually.* Turn to the "What About Me? section at the end of the chapter and complete your individual financial assessments now. Be honest and accurate, because this will show you your true financial status and what needs to be done with it.

2. *Create a budget.* Using the financial assessments you did individually, you can develop a budget for your marriage by turning to the "What About Us?" section and completing the financial-budget worksheet. This will help you establish spending limits as well as set priorities and goals. Your budget should be the control engine of your money-management plan.

3. *Set realistic goals for getting out of debt.* List actions that must be changed to correct or strengthen your financial situation. Set a time limit to accomplish these goals. Remember, it took you a while to get into debt, and it may take longer to get out of it. Pray for patience, and encourage each other to use self-discipline.

4. *To accomplish your goals, you need to set priorities.* Eliminating credit-card debt may be your first priority. Tackle paying off the cards with the highest interest rates first. To stop the misuse of credit cards, you'll need to distinguish carefully between your needs and wants. If you explore why you think you need or want something beforehand, you may be surprised how many wants can be eliminated.

5. *Monitor your progress, especially your spending.* You may be shocked

to recognize that you have some unhealthy spending habits. Establish strict boundaries to begin new healthy money habits. Track daily expenses, down to cups of coffee or candy purchases—they all add up. Two daily trips to Starbucks can cost you hundreds of dollars a month! This will be very informative when you compare income to expenses. If you're short on the income side, you'll know why and see where you need to cut back.

6. *Celebrate (in some reasonable way) when you achieve a financial goal.* You might go out for dinner or just have a dessert date. Find something that you both would enjoy and set aside time to celebrate.

If you have a hard time with financial discipline, join a financial Bible study or a program where you'll have support and accountability. You might also seek out an older couple who can mentor you in financial planning and help you be accountable to keep within your budget.

What's important is your attitude about money, not the amount you have. Without a good plan for wisely managing your money, you may find it almost impossible to control your finances. Freedom from debt requires a tenacious attitude and lots of discipline, as well as a willingness to learn from any financial setbacks that may come your way.

Money should be a source of comfort, not stress, and it can be if you work together to manage your money wisely and find solutions for your problems. Working together on your finances will strengthen the bond between you and build trust, intimacy, and love.

What About Me?

Assess your present financial situation separately before developing a budget for your marriage. Begin by filling in the individual *His* and *Hers* blanks found in the Current Financial Statement/Proposed Budget section beginning on page 125. As you do, you will evaluate how much each of you currently allot to the following categories.

Housing (including rent/mortgage and utilities)

Food

Auto

Tithe

Savings

Debt (school loans/auto loans/home loans)

Insurance (auto/homeowners/medical)

Medical

Clothing

Recreation/entertainment

Miscellaneous

What About Us?

Work together to prepare a financial budget for when you're married. [Note: If you tend to be an impulsive buyer, set a limit for discretionary buying. Limit your purchases to under $50 (or only what you can afford after doing your budget). Anything over that, discuss it together, budget for it, delay your purchase, wait for a sale, or decide not to buy it.]

Suggested budget percentages:

Housing (including rent/mortgage and utilities): 25–30 percent

Food: 10 percent

Auto: 15 percent

Tithe: 10 percent

Savings: 5–10 percent

Debt (school loans/auto loans/home loans): 5 percent

Insurance (auto/homeowners/medical): 5 percent

Medical: 5 percent

Clothing: 5 percent

Recreation/entertainment: 5 percent

Miscellaneous: 5 percent
Total: 100 percent

CURRENT FINANCIAL STATEMENT/PROPOSED BUDGET

Income per Month

			Marriage Budget
Salary	his _____	hers _____	us _____
Other income (interest, dividends, etc.)	his _____	hers _____	us _____
Gross income	his _____	hers _____	us _____
Then subtract:			
Tithe/charitable giving	his _____	hers _____	us _____
Savings	his _____	hers _____	us _____
Other	his _____	hers _____	us _____
Total Income:	**his** _____	**hers** _____	**us** _____

Expenses per Month

Housing:

Rent/mortgage/lease	his _____	hers _____	us _____
Insurance (renter's or house)	his _____	hers _____	us _____
Taxes	his _____	hers _____	us _____
Miscellaneous (repairs, etc.)	his _____	hers _____	us _____

Utilities:

Electricity	his _____	hers _____	us _____
Gas	his _____	hers _____	us _____
Water	his _____	hers _____	us _____

Cable   his _____   hers _____   us _____

Trash   his _____   hers _____   us _____

Internet   his _____   hers _____   us _____

Phone (landline and cell)   his _____   hers _____   us _____

Maintenance/repairs   his _____   hers _____   us _____

Other   his _____   hers _____   us _____

Food:

Groceries   his _____   hers _____   us _____

Eating out   his _____   hers _____   us _____

Auto:

Payments   his _____   hers _____   us _____

Taxes/license   his _____   hers _____   us _____

Gas   his _____   hers _____   us _____

Maintenance/repairs   his _____   hers _____   us _____

Replacement   his _____   hers _____   us _____

Medical:

Doctor   his _____   hers _____   us _____

Dentist   his _____   hers _____   us _____

Pharmacy   his _____   hers _____   us _____

Other   his _____   hers _____   us _____

Insurance:

Life   his _____   hers _____   us _____

Health   his _____   hers _____   us _____

Auto   his _____   hers _____   us _____

Other   his _____   hers _____   us _____

Debts:

Credit cards   his _____   hers _____   us _____

   (record each one)   _____   _____   _____

                          _____   _____   _____

Loans   his _____   hers _____   us _____

Education   his _____   hers _____   us _____
Personal (friends/family)   his _____   hers _____   us _____
Other   his _____   hers _____   us _____

Entertainment:

Movies (theater/video rental)   his _____   hers _____   us _____
Trips   his _____   hers _____   us _____
Activities/sports   his _____   hers _____   us _____
Vacation   his _____   hers _____   us _____
Pets   his _____   hers _____   us _____
Other   his _____   hers _____   us _____

Clothing:

New purchases   his _____   hers _____   us _____
Alterations/dry cleaning   his _____   hers _____   us _____

Miscellaneous:

Beauty/barber   his _____   hers _____   us _____
Toiletries/cosmetics   his _____   hers _____   us _____
Lunch/allowances   his _____   hers _____   us _____
Furniture/household   his _____   hers _____   us _____
Subscriptions/memberships   his _____   hers _____   us _____
Gifts (including Christmas)   his _____   hers _____   us _____
School   his _____   hers _____   us _____
Petty cash   his _____   hers _____   us _____
Emergencies   his _____   hers_____   us _____
Total Expenses: **his** _____   **hers** _____   **us** _____

Income Versus Expenses

Total income   his _____   hers _____   us _____
Less total expenses   his _____   hers _____   us _____
Discretionary funds   his _____   hers _____   us _____
   (hopefully)

Just for Fun!

If you had a million dollars, what charity would you give to and why?

What was the best job you've ever had?

What Does God Say?

There are more than two thousand scriptures that speak about money and possessions, and that means this is a big issue for us—and for God. Here are just a few scriptures:

Wealth and honor come from [the Lord]. (1 Chronicles 29:12)

The wicked borrow and do not repay, but the righteous give generously. (Psalm 37:21)

Dishonest money dwindles away, but he who gathers money little by little makes it grow. (Proverbs 13:11)

All hard work brings a profit, but mere talk leads only to poverty. (Proverbs 14:23)

Better a little with the fear of the LORD than great wealth with turmoil. (Proverbs 15:16)

The plans of the diligent lead to profit as surely as haste leads to poverty. (Proverbs 21:5)

The rich rule over the poor, and the borrower is servant to the lender. (Proverbs 22:7)

Each man should give what he has decided in his heart to give, not reluctantly or under compulsion, for God loves a cheerful giver. (2 Corinthians 9:7)

My God will meet all your needs according to his glorious riches in Christ Jesus. (Philippians 4:19)

Godliness with contentment is great gain. For we brought nothing into the world, and we can take nothing out of it. But if we have food and clothing, we will be content with that. People who want to get rich fall into temptation and a trap and into many foolish and harmful desires that plunge men into ruin and destruction. For the love of money is a root of all kinds of evil. (1 Timothy 6:6–10)

Keep your lives free from the love of money and be content with what you have. (Hebrews 13:5)

9

A Productive Partnership

How Do You Handle the Nitty-Gritty of Daily Life?

From the time you rise in the morning until you fall into bed at night, you're expected to play certain roles, fulfill certain responsibilities, and make hundreds of decisions, large and small. It's the stuff of daily life. But the way you approach each day's tasks makes all the difference in the world.

Growing up, Tim watched his parents fulfill very traditional male and female roles: the man cared for the outside of the home, and the woman cared for the inside. Fortunately for Tim, he and his bride lived in an apartment, and since outside maintenance was taken care of, Tim thought he was off the hook as far as daily duties and responsibilities.

Angie had a different idea about a woman's place in the home and household responsibilities. She'd been raised in a home where Mom and Dad shared it all—cooking, cleaning, laundry, yard work, and so on. When Tim sat in front of the TV night after night and expected

Angie to do all the "inside stuff," she couldn't believe it. She expected equality in the home. In fact, she demanded it by giving Tim a list of all the things she normally did around the house and pointing out how little he contributed.

A heated argument ensued, and Tim dug in his heels. After all, he worked 45 to 50 hours a week, while Angie only had a part-time retail position. As time passed, their marital journey was littered with power games, manipulation, control, and stubborn dissension—until they discovered God's thoughts on the matter.

The division of labor is usually one of the first challenges newlyweds face. How do you get everything done that needs doing in the limited time you have? Who will do which chores? Who will run what errands? Usually, during the newlywed years, both the husband and wife work, so finding time to get chores and errands accomplished often becomes complicated.

So how do you figure out what roles each of you will assume, how you'll delegate responsibilities, and how you'll make decisions? As a child, you watched your parents fulfill different roles. Now, as a soon-to-be-married adult, you must assess your respective roles as husband and wife and decide what will work best in your marriage.

Who's best skilled to accomplish a particular task? Who has the time to run a certain errand? Your goal should be to find a balance and share the workload so as to accomplish life's everyday challenges.

This chapter will help you sort out many of these issues, talk about how you can best handle everyday living, and find ways to balance the details of everyday living in positive and productive ways.

How You Were Programmed

Like Tim and Angie, each of you comes to marriage with personal history and experiences that mold the way you'll think about your role as a husband or a wife and the role of your future spouse. How you were raised and how you saw your parents live daily life will color how you view your role—or your future mate's role.

Cultural expectations also influence the way you think about male and female roles. But besides your role as a spouse, you'll also fulfill other roles after you marry—employee, friend, church member, citizen, adult child, and possibly, parent—and each of these roles will carry its own responsibilities.

What did you learn about the roles of husbands and wives in your church, at your school, or among your friends when you were growing up? You may have heard conflicting ideas of what a wife should do, how she should act, what responsibilities she should assume, and to what extent she should be involved in making decisions. And what about that word *submission*? These views may have left you with a number of questions about a wife's role.

You may also have questions about a husband's role. Should he be the leader in your marriage? If so, why? What about power games, those inevitable struggles for control within a marriage? Should the husband really have to help around the house? And who, ultimately, should make decisions?

Alexi received her psychology degree from a university that had very liberal views of marriage and gender roles. Though as a Christian she fought to maintain her faith in the midst of such moral relativism, the liberal views she had been exposed to in her secular education crept into her marriage with Brent. She just couldn't allow herself to be "ruled" by Brent. She kept her finances separate, refused to allow Brent to make even the simplest decisions, and fought against his desires to protect and care for her. And she definitely wouldn't succumb to the idea that she was his "helper."

Brent, on the other hand, thought leadership meant controlling the situation, so he pushed and demanded that Alexi "submit." Fortunately, it didn't take long for them to realize that they needed some counseling to figure out what was going so wrong. Once they understood God's plan for men and women, they adjusted their thinking accordingly, and their actions soon followed suit.

God's plan for your marriage isn't for you to play power games, manipulate each other to get your way, or control your mate for selfish purposes. According to God's plan, you're here on this earth to love and serve. If that's the case, then your role as a husband or wife will primarily be to love and serve your mate.

We can do that in many ways: by meeting each other's needs, fulfilling each other's realistic expectations, and accepting each other's differences.

The truth is that God made man to naturally be the protector, provider, and covering for his wife and children, as well as the leader and, ultimately, the one responsible for the family. He's not a paycheck, a bill payer, or a convenient roomie—as I [Susan] have heard women quip in the movies and in real life.

God made woman to naturally be a completer, a helper, a counterpart, a nurturer, a balancer, and a life giver. She's not a plaything, a doormat, or a maid—as I've [Dale] seen men treat their wives in real life, on TV shows, and in the movies.

In Ephesians 5:25, the apostle Paul wrote about how a husband should love his wife: "Husbands, love your wives, just as Christ loved the church and gave himself up for her." Guys, when you marry, this should be your vow, your commitment to your wife. You must be willing to sacrifice your life—if need be—as Jesus did for us. While this example is the extreme, the point is that you can no longer continue to be selfish.

The leadership and submission Paul talks about in Ephesians are areas in which both spouses work together as a team, are united, serve each other, defer to one another, and have the same goals. Though the leader is the one responsible to see the signs ahead and respond accordingly, both you and your future mate need to stop and pay attention to the dangers before proceeding—as you would when you come to a yield sign. You must also encourage each other, support one another, and keep the enthusiasm going so you won't get weary or feel as though one of you is doing most of the work. It comes

ontoured
, ¾" browband,
with ⅝" fancy
eins. Hook-stud
l) or 3 (Oversize).

r Bridle   **$520.00**
ng Martingale   **$200.00**

Ultra-luxe nubuck seat

⭐⭐⭐⭐⭐

5 stars (over 20 reviews)

"It rides like a dream *and makes you really feel secure. Worth the money.*"

— *Sarah I. from Darlington, SC*

ès NC Jumping Saddle

When top riders demand the latest technology, uncompromising performance, and
s saddle rises to the challenge. Made for all jumping disciplines, this saddle integrates
nto a design for horse and rider comfort. Sit in this saddle once and you'll never settle
rolls, seat and panels with grain flaps. Panels are lined with a shock absorbing foam.
s. Medium-deep seat and medium tree. 16½ in Short or Regular flap. 17 in Regular or
gular, Long or Long/Forward flap. 18 in Long/Forward or Extra Long/Forward flap.
ow twist. 17½ and 18 have regular twist. Note: Does not include custom fitting.

Over $75

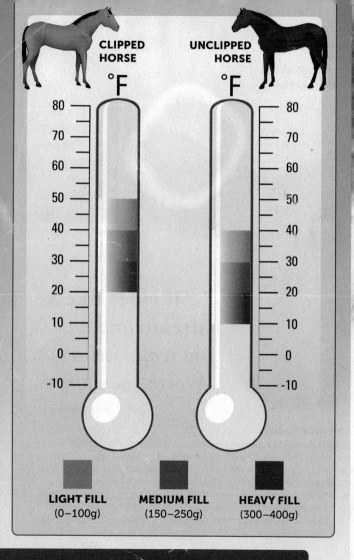

CLIPPED HORSE °F

UNCLIPPED HORSE °F

LIGHT FILL (0–100g)

MEDIUM FILL (150–250g)

HEAVY FILL (300–400g)

down to three things: teamwork, being a servant to each other, and avoiding the power games that will hurt your marriage.

FINDING THE BALANCE

The roles of a man and woman are unique, but they're also of equal value in God's eyes. Here's a great metaphor we recently heard: Marriage is like a tandem bike. The lead rider and the co-rider work together as equals for a common goal as they stay in sync with each other. They pedal toward the same

Ask the Expert

Down the road in your marriage, you may need light remodeling, minor repair, or major reconstruction. In his book *Blueprints for a Solid Marriage*, Dr. Steve Stephens writes,

> No marriage is perfect, but every marriage can be improved. Marriages fall apart because needs are not met. . . . Some of these might be major needs and some minor, but all of them are important. The ones which are most important to him might not be the most important to her. Yet the more areas of your house you feel good about, the better you feel about the whole house.[1]

No matter how long you've been together, every marriage can benefit from some fun extracurricular activities to keep the romance alive. *Blueprints for a Solid Marriage* helps time-strapped couples quickly assess and enhance their relationships with a detailed plan for marriage-improvement projects.

destination, but the leader steers the bike, provides the steady pace, protects them from potential danger, and works with the co-rider to reach their destination. They must stay balanced, or they'll fall. They must stay in sync and connected as a team, or they'll crash. They must communicate with and adjust to each other, or they'll have problems.

It's also important to note what leadership isn't: it's not overpowering, controlling, or dominating. If you have a controlling leader on a tandem bike, the co-rider will soon grow weary, become discouraged, and feel very unsafe. If either of you currently feels this way in your relationship, or if there's an abuse of power, you should talk with a counselor right away to resolve this important issue.

SCHEDULING CHALLENGES

In chapter 6 we talked about the importance of slowing down and making time to communicate with each other. If you let it, this busy world will hinder good times of connecting and communicating that you could have with your future mate. Overloaded schedules will undoubtedly increase the stress within marriage. So it's important to begin your life together by reevaluating your schedules and prioritizing in ways that are satisfactory to both of you.

Tina and Will had full-time jobs and lots of scheduled activities with their two children and a multitude of friends. The problem was, they didn't make enough time for each other. After work they ran their children to several sports and other activities, kept up with extended family and friends, even volunteered for several events at church and their children's school. By the end of the day, they hardly had energy to say good night, let alone share their lives through good communication or intimacy. Because of this, as time went by, Tina and Will had very little in common emotionally, socially, spiritually, or in any other area, and their relationship rarely reached levels of true intimacy.

How can you avoid the pitfalls of overscheduling and overcommitting yourselves as a couple? A good place to start is by looking at your priorities. Healthy priorities should align with God's priorities for your life—God, spouse, family, work, in that order—if you want maximum rewards of a great marriage. And your priorities as a couple should be compatible. One of you can't decide to hang out with your single friends every weekend while the other sits home alone. Compromise and come to a mutual agreement, realizing that sometimes you may need to get counsel from others.

As time passes and your lives change, additional responsibilities and duties will inevitably come. That's why it's so important now to understand the value of setting aside time to connect, communicate, and be available when you need each other.

And as you address the roles, responsibilities, duties, and decisions of daily life, work together as a team to get tasks, chores, and jobs done in a fair and appropriate manner. This will make your daily lives peaceful, pleasant, and productive.

BE-ATTITUDES OF DAILY LIVING

So how do you make all of this happen? How do you get daily jobs done, complete those boring, mundane duties, and accomplish every chore, in the midst of your busy day, while staying in harmony with each other? It's all about attitude!

We all get weary doing those mundane tasks of life. But just like when you were a kid and had to clean up your room or do the dishes or take out the trash, tackling everyday chores as a couple is about the attitude you have toward those chores. And even more, it's about your attitude toward each other.

Every Saturday morning, Maggie and Dean plan their chores for the day. "Divide and conquer" is the operative phrase for them. Though Dean enjoys caring for the car and jumps at the chance when it's needed, it's not always a necessity. So he pitches in to do whatever needs to be done. Sometimes it's running errands and doing the grocery shopping; at other times it's cleaning toilets and vacuuming. This couple sees their to-do list as a team project.

Here are eight "be-attitudes" that Maggie and Dean use to make every-day chores and duties a breeze:

- *Be positive.* Set priorities by determining what's most important and why it's important. Don't sweat the small stuff. If you tackle mundane chores with a positive attitude and sacrificial enthusiasm, that'll be half the battle.

- *Be unselfish.* Pull your own weight. Don't expect your future mate to do all or even most of the work. Step up to the plate and do your fair share. On the other hand, don't keep score if you feel you're pulling more of the load. Adjust when needed.

- *Be willing to use your skills and abilities.* Use your strengths. If he's a good cook and she's a good mechanic, go for it. Don't feel tied to traditional duties. Use each other's skills to your mutual benefit.

- *Be a team.* Take on jobs as a team—"divide and conquer." Just be sure to choose duties together and compromise when necessary.

- *Be servants.* Just as Jesus washed the disciples' feet when they least expected it, serve your future mate by doing a chore without him or her knowing about it or by making dinner when he or she has had a tough day.

- *Be content.* You know there will always be things that need to be done, but avoid becoming discontent and grumbling about what's inevitable. Chores are a part of life.

- *Be adaptable to the changes of life.* When one of you is sick or working extra hours, pick up the slack for him or her for a while.

- *Be careful to use time management.* We can always put off those mundane, boring things, but they'll just pile up and get worse. Manage your time so you can deal with chores on a daily or weekly basis, and you'll be better off.

A DEMOCRACY OR A DICTATORSHIP?

As busy as Stu and Holly were, in order to get things done, this young couple decided to be proactive about making daily decisions. In just one week, they made decisions not only about what meals to make and what clothes to wear but also about Sunday's tithe, Monday's sports night and meeting, Tuesday's bill-paying session, Wednesday's dinner guests, Thursday's movie choice, Friday's date-night destination, and Saturday's shopping and chore lists.

Part of daily living is making the many decisions you have to make each and every day. Besides deciding on chores, tasks, and duties, you need to make the inevitable decisions about finances—what to buy, how much to save, and so on. How will you spend your time together and apart? What decisions will you make about spiritual things, such as what church to attend, moral stands, tithing, and charitable giving? Who gets the line-item veto or final say in a decision that's hard to resolve?

There are also major decisions, such as where to live and work and when to have children. There are fearful decisions, such as whether to have elective surgery. And there are minor decisions, such as what to have for dinner. Each decision should be given the appropriate weight and as much (or as little) time as it deserves.

You'll sometimes make a wrong decision, together or separately—that's just part of life. So admit when you've made an error, forgive each other, learn from your mistakes, and avoid blaming your future mate.

Soon after we married, Dale noticed a spot on my [Susan's] nose and suggested we get it examined. I was afraid and procrastinated getting it checked, but when I finally did see the doctor, I found out it was cancer! Dale and I had to decide what to do, especially since the surgery could have scarred me for life. Making that decision together gave me strength to do what needed to be done, and although the surgery was much more extensive than I ever imagined it would be, Dale's love and strength helped me through it all.

Because we made the decision together and were in complete agreement about our course of action, we journeyed through the trauma of several months of recovery in harmony and security.

No matter how big or small a decision may be, as a couple you should try your best to come to a mutual agreement on the things you must decide. To do this, you must use your communication skills, you must cooperate, and sometimes you must compromise. The key is to work as a team to come to a mutual decision that will work for both of you.

What About Me?

Think about each of the following questions, and then discuss them with your future mate:

- What did your father's role look like? Your mother's role?
- Do you think your parents were healthy emotionally and relationally? Why or why not?
- How do you feel about how your parents related to each other?
- How did your parents make decisions? Did they talk about decisions together or did one spouse make decisions without consulting his or her mate?
- What would you like to see your roles as husband and wife look like?
- How would you like to make decisions as a couple once you're married?

What About Us?

Now it's time to talk about what you both expect regarding the division of household chores, errands, tasks, and duties. Remember what we said earlier: Divvy up your responsibilities according to your strengths and your schedules. And keep in mind that while this checklist is a baseline to get you started, you should both be flexible. There will be times when you'll have to step up for your future mate or adjust your duties according to schedule changes.

Who will do the following chores?

- Cooking and preparing meals
- Cleaning up after meals
- Cleaning bathrooms
- Doing the laundry
- Taking out the trash
- Grocery shopping
- Decorating
- Taking care of household repairs
- Servicing the car
- Doing the yard work
- Planning trips
- Planning nights out
- Buying and giving gifts
- Planning and shopping for holidays
- Corresponding with family and friends
- Caring for aging parents
- Caring for pets

Just for Fun!

What types of chores did you do as a child?

What was the name of your first pet?

What Does God Say?

Read the following scriptures and discuss how they relate to everyday married life:

I have set you an example that you should do as I have done for you. I tell you the truth, no servant is greater than his master, nor is a messenger greater than the one who sent him. (John 13:15–16)

Be imitators of God, therefore, as dearly loved children and live a life of love, just as Christ loved us and gave himself up for us as a fragrant offering and sacrifice to God. (Ephesians 5:1)

Submit to one another out of reverence for Christ. (Ephesians 5:21)

Do nothing out of selfish ambition or vain conceit, but in humility consider others better than yourselves. Each of you should look not only to your own interests, but also to the interests of others. (Philippians 2:3–4)

Husbands, in the same way be considerate as you live with your wives, and treat them with respect . . . as heirs with you of the gracious gift of life, so that nothing will hinder your prayers. (1 Peter 3:7)

THE INTIMATE MYSTERY
What's God's Design for Sexual Intimacy?

Last summer Dale and I [Susan] enjoyed a little piece of paradise as we camped along Clear Creek in the Rocky Mountains. The river roared with strength as it tumbled over boulders bigger than cars. The sun sparkled on the rapids, giving the water life as it moved from mountaintops to lakes and reservoirs below. It was wonderful to enjoy its beauty and power.

But it was also dangerous, for if we had accidentally fallen in, we surely would have met our deaths from the sheer force of the turbulent waters. Or if the river had left its banks, it would have brought destruction and devastation.

So it is with sex. The sex drive is one of the strongest instincts we have, and within the boundaries of marriage, it's beautiful, life giving, and wonderful. But when it leaves its rightful place, or if we engage in it at the wrong time, it can be destructive and dangerous.

God made it that way, and He gave us an owner's manual with specific instructions regarding enjoying the intimacy of sex within marriage.

Sex within marriage is a reflection of unselfish giving, not unlike the loving relationship Christ has with His church. It's about care, sacrifice, devotion, tenderness, and respect. It's about fun, pleasure, enjoyment, and the reality of experiencing true intimacy. And it's also fulfilling, honorable, healthy, and healing.

Although you already know a lot about your future mate, the reality is, you'll spend the rest of your life getting to know him or her better. But in areas as deep and intimate as sex, understanding how your future mate is wired is very important.

WE'RE INTELLIGENTLY DESIGNED

God made us for each other, and when we love, serve, and enjoy one another as He planned, sex is awesome beyond words.

His plan for sex in marriage includes multiple purposes:

- Procreation (We're part of His creation plan to bring new life into being.)
- Holy living (We're to keep sex exclusively within marriage.)
- True intimacy (He wants us to experience communication, companionship, and understanding at the deepest levels.)
- True fulfillment (We enjoy giving and receiving pleasure, comfort, release, and fun through sexual intimacy.)

When God created Adam and Eve, they were purposefully and clearly different from each other, yet they were also complementary—physically, emotionally, and in every other way. No doubt they experienced real intimacy through openness, honesty, safety, and transparency. Remember, the Bible says they were naked but not ashamed (Genesis 2:25).

But after the Fall, Adam and Eve covered themselves and hid from their Creator, obviously feeling ashamed and unsafe. Their sin changed the way they related to each other and to God—spiritually, emotionally, intellectually, and even physically.

Selfish disobedience does that to all of us. It brings guilt, mistrust, isolation, and fear of being close, just as it did with Adam and Eve. But selflessness and sacrifice build intimacy. And controlling your sexual desires until they can be freely expressed within marriage is God's design. Saving sex for marriage teaches you how to harness other desires, sinful or not, so you can live a life of self-control.

How Did You Learn About Sex?

Take a moment and consider where your attitudes about sex came from. Your parents? Teachers? Friends? Older siblings? Television shows, movies, music, or other media? Pornography?

Are there unhealthy things you learned or experienced in your family? Was sex considered taboo, or did you learn that sex was the way to make up for bad behavior? Were dirty jokes or pornography permitted in your house? Were there double standards in your home—were the guys free to be promiscuous but the girls expected to remain chaste? Did sex seem like a duty to one or both of your parents, or did you sense that your parents' relationship was fulfilling and unselfish?

Jake grew up in a family where pornography was openly accepted. His father had subscriptions to *Playboy* and other "girlie" magazines, and his mother apparently said nothing. The garage was filled with centerfolds, so Jake and his friends spent lots of time in that garage, exposed to images that quickly became imprinted on their minds—images that formed the boys' views of what a woman should look and be like sexually.

By the time Jake married Barb, he was already addicted to online pornography and patronized strip clubs. His unhealthy behavior continued after they married, but it wasn't long until the marriage began falling apart. The sexual dysfunction, distrust, betrayal, and heartache cost both of them dearly. Now separated from Barb, Jake realizes the price of such addictions and is determined to get the help he needs. He hopes it's not too late to heal their broken marriage.

Growing up, you might have picked up on a range of attitudes about sex not only from your family but from teachers, peers, and the media. You may have picked up on any of the following:

- Unfaithfulness is common.
- Sex is embarrassing.
- Sex is a topic for teasing and joking.
- Viewing pornography is fine.
- Sex is fearful.
- Public expressions of affection are unacceptable.
- Recreational sex is acceptable.
- Condom usage protects against STDs (sexually transmitted diseases) and AIDS.

All of these attitudes will affect the way you view sex, so understanding the good and the bad things you've learned from others about sex is important. You may have strong feelings about oral sex, foreplay, negligees, petting, bathing together, or the need for cleanliness. Think about these things and assess why you feel the way you do about each topic.

If either of you was promiscuous or involved in recreational sex in your past, confessing your moral failure is important, but specific details of your past sexual history typically don't need to be discussed. You should, however, make sure you're sensitive and honest with your future mate so that any dangerous behaviors, or the consequences thereof (STDs, HIV-AIDS, etc.), can be resolved medically and/or emotionally. The truth is that premarital sexual experiences of any kind may bring unhealthy habits into your marriage, so it's best to be honest with your future mate from the beginning.

Issues such as sexual abuse, incest, molestation, homosexual experiences, promiscuity, or a pornography addiction may require that you and/or your future mate engage in therapy with a professional counselor. Other troubling sexual experiences may be settled in a brief session with your pastor or a counselor, with or without your future spouse, so that healing can hopefully be achieved. Know that with God's forgiveness and love, there's hope for those who have failed in this area or who have had harmful or hurtful experiences.

Sheila should have gotten counseling before she married. She was molested as a child but never dealt with the emotional effects of what happened to her. The shame of the molestation experience and her later promiscuity affected her marriage greatly because her view of sex was so distorted. Today her husband is frustrated, and their marriage is in constant crisis because she still hasn't gotten the help she needs. If you've been a victim of any kind of sexual molestation or abuse, don't hide or ignore this problem and its aftereffects. Get the professional help you need.

WHY WAIT?

The simple truth is, sex outside of marriage hinders intimacy. It's a myth that only masquerades as love and intimacy.

If you're already sexually active with each other, we urge you to stop and sincerely ask God and your partner for forgiveness. Then make a vow with each other to remain abstinent until you marry. If you're living together, we strongly suggest that one of you move out and that you both change your lifestyles. Take time to get to know each other without sexual involvement and the daily intimacy of living in the same place, and make sure that you're both unshackled from the past.

You may be afraid that if you choose to stop having premarital sex, your future mate will feel hurt or, worse, decide to end the relationship. This could happen, of course, but if it did, it would tell you that your future mate is marrying you for the wrong reasons. It's more likely that he or she will only have greater respect for you, for your future mate will see that you value him or her more than sexual gratification.

Waiting also builds trust, confidence, loyalty, and bonding. Matthew 5:8 says, "Blessed are the pure in heart, for they will see God." That includes purity in the way you dress, think, and behave.

Though it's hard, flee from tempting and overstimulating situations.

You're attracted to each other, and you should be, but don't stoke the fires until your wedding night. It may be helpful to limit your private time together and instead do things with others. Avoid setting the mood or engaging in activities that will likely encourage sexual intimacy. Respect the one you love enough to keep him or her chaste until you marry.

Since sin begins in the mind, set boundaries on what you think, watch, read, see, say, and listen to. Don't put yourself in vulnerable situations; being

Ask the Experts

In their book *The Way to Love Your Wife: Creating Greater Love and Passion in the Bedroom*, Clifford and Joyce Penner write,

> A lot of men find it tough to take directions even when they're lost. How much more difficult to take directions from your wife about sex! Yet sex works better when the man lets the woman set the pace. Solomon, a model of the sexually satisfied man, let his bride lead their physical relationship—as you'll see in this book. And Christ, the model of unselfish love, gave up His rights for His bride, the church.[1]

Once you're married, the Penners' book is a great resource to help you grow in your sexual relationship. It's a guide to having great sex by working together as you share common goals for achieving sexual intimacy as a couple. You'll learn more about your bodies, how to develop good communication about sex, and ways to overcome sexual difficulties that may arise. The Penners also point out sexual pitfalls and suggest ways to be creative and discover each other's sexuality. Sex is God's gift for married couples to enjoy without shame or guilt.

alone with your future mate in some settings or going to inappropriate places are temptations you don't need to deal with. Be accountable to someone you respect and trust, and make sure your future mate shares your beliefs about this.

LOOKING FORWARD

If you're planning to marry in the near future, it may be time to discuss your future intimacy with each other. Don't try it; just discuss it!

How can you tell—before marriage—if your partner has the same interest, attitude, and desire for sex as you do? The first indicator might be physical attraction, that spark you feel, the sense of excitement, the magnetism—what some call infatuation. Later it may be how you hold hands, hold each other, or kiss. God made you sensitive and discerning enough to know if your partner is romantically inclined and/or just sexually interested.

God made man and woman sexually compatible, and barring any physical or psychological problems, sex is almost instinctive. Therefore, unlike what the culture or media says, you don't have to try it first to know if or how it works. If your future spouse is kind, giving, unselfish, and seeking your best interest, sex will be, most likely, a joyful journey of discovery.

Sex is about connecting and relating on the most intimate level. After you're married, you'll have the joy of getting to know each other on a much deeper, intimate level—emotionally, sexually, and spiritually. Sex brings two people into a deep, loving bond through passion and joy.

Although sex is rather instinctive to both men and women, it's still a complex journey of understanding your own sexuality as well as your spouse's. If you don't have a full understanding of your physical body and sexual makeup, consider reading the Penners' book. Men and women view sex differently, and it's important for each of you to understand these differences.

Women tend to be verbally centered. What they hear matters. A husband should regularly affirm his wife for who she is as a person and tell her how much he admires her physically. A woman is stimulated by touch, is aroused by tender words, and needs time to relax so she can enjoy sex. She requires a gradual buildup during sex but doesn't always need orgasm to feel fulfilled.

Ultimately, a man's fulfillment should be found when his wife is sexually satisfied, and to do that, he must focus on her feelings. When she feels honored and cherished, she will be more giving, and you'll both feel satisfied.

On the other hand, men are usually visually centered. What they see matters, so a wife should try to be attractive and available to her husband. It's helpful if she regularly affirms him personally for what he does, as well as

Preparing for Marital Sex

Six to eight weeks before the wedding, we suggest you do the following:

- Schedule a doctor's appointment for a physical (and pelvic exam for women). If you've been sexually active, get tested for STDs and HIV.
- Discuss birth control and plans for children with your future spouse and your doctor.
- Discuss what you think might be your sexual needs, likes, and dislikes, as well as when and how often you might want to enjoy sexual intimacy.
- Study anything you're unsure about regarding male and female sexuality and physiology.
- Seek professional counseling if any of the following concerns you:
  1. Memories or consequences of past promiscuity
  2. Pornography addiction
  3. Problems such as sexual abuse, shame, fear, and guilt.

compliments him physically. Since a man finds pleasure through sexual release, he usually needs orgasm to feel fulfilled.

For some people, the transition of going from an abstinence mentality to a have-at-it mentality isn't always easy. Couples who have saved themselves for marriage and have tried to be careful about their thoughts and behaviors are suddenly expected to be just the opposite with each other. So spouses should be patient and understanding with one another during the adjustment process.

How do you make this transition? "You have to realize that now you're free to enjoy intimacy the way God intended," admits a friend of ours. "It's all about recognizing that it's not only okay; it's good."

It's an intricate dance, to be sure. It takes each of you seeking to please the other, but that's the joy of it. Sex is an all-encompassing act; it involves your physical, mental, emotional, and spiritual selves. God wants you to have fun, to be free to indulge in sex, unashamed of who you are or how He made each of you. Sex connects husband and wife on the deepest levels possible, to make you completely safe and vulnerable together, and to allow you to experience a unique closeness only with each other.

SEX IS TO BE ENJOYED!

Intimacy comes when you trust each other completely on the deepest levels. As you share your feelings, thoughts, fears, and joys regarding sex, you'll build trust, security, acceptance, and caring. So how do you achieve this?

- Be sure you're comfortable and safe with each other's sexuality, knowing that sex is a wonderful gift provided for your joy and pleasure.
- Understand what pleases each other. How often would you like to make love? What makes your spouse feel treasured (gifts, outings, companionship, quality time, interests, experiences, affirmation, cards, letters, calls, dates, getaways, surprises, physical touch, compliments, tenderness, etc.)?

- Once married, take note of each other's needs, wants, fears, and desires. What pleases, excites, honors, and creates security, passion, and freedom? What touch, word, sight, or sound creates desire? Be careful not to be too goal oriented; just enjoy the experience and celebrate the relationship. Don't expect perfection—or routine—in your sex life; love each other and have fun.
- As you grow in your sexual relationship, build variety into it. Besides enjoying your normal ways of making love, be adventurous and open to enjoying new places, positions, and experiences. Enjoy foreplay, take your time—unless it's a quickie—and celebrate the passion, freedom, and enjoyment of intimacy.
- Protect your marriage. Keep your sexual relationship private. Don't talk about the specifics with others (unless it's a professional counselor).
- Change with time and seasons, and when necessary, forgive and move on. Make your sex life a priority and set aside time for it. Make your life together an exciting new adventure.
- Be mindful that sexual intimacy is a sacred act because our bodies are temples created by God (1 Corinthians 6:19). There's absolutely no better way to bond and connect with your spouse.

There it is! Sex shouldn't be such a mystery after all. God created sex to be enjoyed.

Making love is a lifelong learning experience—it's a process of building intimacy physically, emotionally, psychologically, and spiritually. Your sexual desires will ebb and flow—sometimes they will be stronger and other times weaker—and they will be different for each of you. Job stress, fatigue, health problems, and so on can all have an effect on your desire (or lack thereof) for sex. That's normal. And remember, if any issues or problems arise in this area, don't let embarrassment keep you from getting professional help.

Sex is a deep nonverbal expression of love that can only be fully realized in an atmosphere of safety and commitment. Sexual intimacy involves the mind, will, emotions, and body working together within the context of the intimate relationship you're developing throughout the rest of your life together. It's also fun, holy, exciting, and life changing. Enjoy!

What About Me?

Answer the following questions individually. You may want to discuss some of your responses with your future mate when you discuss the "What About Us?" questions.

- What was your family's attitude about sex?
- How did you first learn about sex?
- What experiences and influences from your childhood and adolescence might hinder healthy sex with your future mate?
- Do you understand the physiology of your own body and your future mate's body?
- Are you comfortable talking about sex? Why or why not?
- How has the media and culture influenced what you think about sex?
- How comfortable are you with your body? Your appearance?
- How important is healthy sex to you and your future mate?

What About Us?

Discuss the following questions together. Add any from the "What About Me?" section that you'd like to ask your future mate.

- On a scale of one to five (one being least important and five being most important), how important is sex to you?
- How will I know if you want sex or just closeness?
- What worries do you have about sex?
- Can we both initiate sex?
- What is your attitude about giving or receiving sexual pleasure?

- Are there limits? Acts or behaviors that aren't okay to you?
- What would ruin sexual intimacy for you?
- What would make sex really good for you?

Just for Fun!

What would you name your firstborn son?

What would you name your firstborn daughter?

What Does God Say?

Read the following scriptures that describe God's purposes for sexual intimacy:

1. Procreation:

So God created man in his own image, in the image of God he created him; male and female he created them.

God blessed them and said to them, "Be fruitful and increase in number." (Genesis 1:27–28)

Sons are a heritage from the LORD, children a reward from him. Like arrows in the hands of a warrior are sons born in one's youth. Blessed is the man whose quiver is full of them. (Psalm 127:3–5)

2. Recreation:

Enjoy life with your wife, whom you love, all the days of this meaningless life that God has given you under the sun. (Ecclesiastes 9:9)

How delightful is your love, my sister, my bride! How much more pleasing is your love than wine. (Song of Songs 4:10)

3. Communication:

The LORD God said, "It is not good for the man to be alone. I will make a helper suitable for him." (Genesis 2:18)

4. Enjoying true intimacy:

For this reason a man will leave his father and mother and be united to his wife, and they will become one flesh. (Genesis 2:24)

May your fountain be blessed, and may you rejoice in the wife of your youth. A loving doe, a graceful deer—may her breasts satisfy you always, may you ever be captivated by her love. (Proverbs 5:18–19)

5. Companionship:

If a man has recently married, he must not be sent to war or have any other duty laid on him. For one year he is to be free to stay at home and bring happiness to the wife he has married. (Deuteronomy 24:5)

Let us go early to the vineyards to see if the vines have budded, if their blossoms have opened, and if the pomegranates are in bloom—there I will give you my love. (Song of Songs 7:12)

6. Purity:

Blessed are the pure in heart, for they will see God. (Matthew 5:8)

[The older women] can train the younger women to love their husbands and children, to be self-controlled and pure, . . . so that no one will malign the word of God. (Titus 2:4–5)

Marriage should be honored by all, and the marriage bed kept pure, for God will judge the adulterer and all the sexually immoral. (Hebrews 13:4)

7. Pleasure:

The husband should fulfill his marital duty to his wife, and likewise the wife to her husband. The wife's body does not belong to her alone but also to her husband. In the same way, the husband's body does not belong to him alone but also to his wife. (1 Corinthians 7:3–4)

After you're married, read the Song of Songs together. It's a book of love, passion, and intimacy.

11

It's a Family Affair

Why Is Family Such a Challenge?

In the movie *My Big Fat Greek Wedding*, Toula and Ian had some interesting challenges when they chose to marry and form their own new family. They came from very different family backgrounds, so the parents of each side—as well as the extended family—had differing expectations for the wedding. And from wedding invitations to bridesmaids' dresses to religious practices, this couple had family involvement. The constant expectations and different opinions placed lots of pressure on this young couple. How would they navigate those challenges? And how would they find a life of their own in the midst of complex family dynamics?

By the end of the movie, this couple discovered a way through the maze of in-law issues. And at the wedding reception, Toula's father said regarding blending the two families, "We're apples and oranges, but in the end, we're all fruit!"

In-laws and extended family can bring many benefits to a marriage. Many in-laws try very hard to love their new daughter-in-law or son-in-law, support the marriage, and maintain healthy boundaries. And extended families bring history, community, and a sense of continuity and identity. The support and love of families can also help a couple become an independent, successful new family.

While the challenges that may come with in-laws can bring stress, they don't have to cause undue concern. Learning what those challenges might be and planning ahead will help you make a smooth transition in forming your own family. When differences between you and your in-laws are discovered, discussed, and accepted, your chances for a happy, healthy marriage will be greatly increased.

WHAT'S THE BIG DEAL?

In-law personalities and interaction can vary greatly from one set of in-laws to another. One set might not want to let their "baby" go, while the other may be a bit jealous of the new relationship. One may demand that everything stay the way it's always been—close, in constant contact, in control—while another freely lets the couple grow as a new family. Or maybe your future spouse doesn't currently have a good relationship with his or her parents. In this case the in-laws might be uninvolved or seem detached.

There will undoubtedly be misunderstandings, hurt feelings, fears, moments of anxiety, strained communication, or unreasonable expectations with and from your in-laws. That's just how it is with relationships. But hopefully those moments will be few, and they don't have to affect your relationship negatively.

You and your in-laws may face communication gaps or differences in the way you view financial assistance or career decisions, life changes or health issues, family closeness, or choices you make. Your in-laws may struggle with how to adjust to the changes your new family brings, with the distance between you and them if you move far away, with how often you communicate, or with the way you connect to them. Your in-laws may have control issues, have inflexible attitudes about carrying on family traditions, or even misunderstand your beliefs.

You and your in-laws may have differing ideas about holidays, family reunions, rearing children, time spent with extended family, interpersonal issues with divorced or blended-family members, responsibility for aging parents, and so much more. All of these can cause in-law challenges. But again, they can be navigated successfully if you work together. Working with your in-laws to resolve conflicts can be a healthy thing to do and can bring you into the family fold like nothing else can. So instead of fearing these challenges, embrace them as a way to learn more about your in-laws and come to love them for who they are.

The truth is that you can't choose your in-laws. So it's best to accept and respect them for being the ones who brought your future spouse into the world and raised him or her.

Attitude is everything when it comes to interpersonal relationships, especially relationships as intimate as those with in-laws and extended families, as well as your future spouse's relationship with his or her family of origin. Don't expect your future mate's family to be like your family and do things the way your family has always done them.

After all is said and done, you're choosing to become a part of your future mate's family when you marry him or her. So how can you become a successful son-in-law or daughter-in-law? Following are six steps that can help you make your in-law relationship successful.

1. Learn all you can about your families. The first step is for you and your future spouse to honestly discuss your in-laws and extended family. Little should surprise you as newlyweds, especially when it comes to family. Your future in-laws may affect your relationship more than you realize, so discuss the differences you see and agree on a plan for how you'll deal with the challenges you may encounter. This includes discussing the positive and negative traits of each of your parents as well as any family matters that may affect your marriage. Don't be defensive or judgmental; simply tell your future mate the truth about your family situation.

Different customs or faiths, moral or ethical issues, and traditions or habits can be challenging, so proactively discuss how to work through those differences as a couple. One or both of your parents may even be facing marital, legal, or financial problems. Any of these problems will likely affect your relationship to some degree, so be aware of the issues and discuss possible solutions for dealing with them.

If your parents are aging or have health issues, talk about possible challenges you may encounter in the future.

Some unhealthy family patterns can be frightening, especially if one or both of you came from an alcoholic or abusive background. Talk honestly about patterns you don't want to repeat in your marriage. If you have family members who are struggling with addictions, talk with your future mate about setting appropriate boundaries to protect your marriage. You may need counseling before or after marriage if you encounter difficult situations involving these family members.

Jessie and Beth both came from dysfunctional families. Fortunately, they were wise enough to discuss their family situations before they married, and they continued to honestly communicate after they married. Even though they had prepared as much as they could, they frequently encountered issues with Jessie's alcoholic mother, Beth's abusive father, and several prodigal siblings who frequently needed a place to stay in between job losses or relational trials. Fortunately, because Jessie and Beth were united in their plans to deal with these challenges and they drew appropriate boundaries, the dysfunctional family members rarely negatively affected their marriage.

If both of you are aware of the issues your families have, and you plan to deal with whatever comes your way as a team, this will help in the adjustment to relating to extended family.

Your parents may also have different philosophies about having or raising children. Be aware of those differences and plan accordingly for the future so you can understand your parents' beliefs and maintain respect for them while still setting appropriate boundaries.

Most important, remember where your loyalty should be once you marry: with your spouse. You won't always be able to please your future spouse and your parents at the same time, so support your future mate and be united in whatever stand you take.

It's also good to learn not to take things too seriously. Romans 12:18 says, "If it is possible, as far as it depends on you, live at peace with everyone." Remember that no one has a perfect family, so give your relatives and in-laws grace to be who they are.

2. Build your in-law relationships. If possible, meet your future in-laws before the wedding week. Far too many couples wait until this hurried, stressful time to finally meet the families they will be related to.

Go to your future in-laws' home, if you can, so you can experience how they live. Your mission is to understand where your future mate came from and to see what the relationship with his or her parents is really like. As you get to know your future in-laws, you'll be seeing a piece of your fiancé(e)'s history.

Parents are on the same mission; they want to know you. Value your time together. Caring parents usually have expectations and opinions, and they're often protective of their child, no matter how old that child might be. So when they ask tough questions, don't be defensive. Try to see things through their eyes, be respectful, and be open as you let them into your life.

Listen to your future in-laws. What are their interests? What things are important to them? Sometimes you'll think you have little in common with them, but don't give up. Find out why they love their son or daughter. Remember, you love the same person they do, so affirm that. You'll see how they view their child, and you'll find it educational and interesting. They'll learn about you too.

When talking about your desires concerning the upcoming wedding, holidays, or other collaborative events, be respectful, honest, and diplomatic. Be careful not to demand your way without considering the input of both your families. Think about what's important to them, but ultimately, do what's best for your marriage.

Good manners are also important, so be polite. A handwritten note will go a long way, especially in today's world where people seldom receive such things.

Even before she was engaged, Johanna wrote a thank-you note to Paul's parents, commending them for all the work they had done in shaping him into a godly, respectable man. Then, when she joined them for a family gathering for the first time, she made a point to help clean up after dinner at her future in-laws' home. She also expressed her thanks and appreciation for their hospitality and the help they offered in planning the wedding. These kinds of gestures can help build a solid relationship with your future in-laws.

Sometimes it's just tough to connect with in-laws. One couple we know said they both have a hard time returning an "I love you" to their respective in-laws. You may also struggle with what to call your in-laws. Ask them what they'd like to be called, and respect their wishes if you can. If your in-laws prefer for you to call them Mom and Dad and you feel comfortable with this, go for it. If not, engage in a healthy discussion to find a solution that works for all of you.

You may feel the same awkwardness and struggle regarding issues of intimacy between you and your in-laws, so focus on developing a strong relationship with them over time. Make a point to stay in touch regularly with them. Call just to say hello. If one or both sets of parents are tech savvy and like to use e-mail, consider connecting with them electronically. This is a fast and easy way to say hello and send pictures or updates. Whatever avenues you choose, keep your in-laws connected to your family as much as possible through regular communication.

3. Form your new family first. Setting priorities outright regarding in-laws and extended families is important for starting your new family. What are your expectations about how you will interact with your in-laws? What are your future mate's expectations?

When Betsy and Carl married, they lived near his parents, so there was a lot of pressure to meet his parents' demands and his extended family members' expectations. The stress, conflict, and frustrations they faced because of this caused many difficult moments early in their marriage. In fact, they didn't feel as though they had really established their own family until they moved away several years after they married.

Parents undoubtedly have expectations, but often the adult child may see things very differently, and that's a recipe for conflict. When you marry, you see yourself as a mature adult, but your parents may not see you that way. One young man we know has the continual challenge of having his father remind him to get enough sleep, wear a coat, even eat right—and he's been married for several years and has a child of his own! This father still doesn't see him as a man; to him, his son is still "daddy's little boy." It's your responsibility—even more than your parents'—to set appropriate boundaries.

It's important to realize that you're forming your *own* family, taking the best of each family of origin, as well as the best of other families you've admired, and beginning your *own* new special traditions in your own family. Yes, parents and extended family are attached to you and your future mate, but when you marry, your mate must come first. You should no longer go to your parents first for advice, counsel, or guidance. Your parents are no longer your primary family, mentors or confidants; your spouse is. It's a new day, a new family, a new life.

4. Prepare for holiday differences. Holidays offer a great time for families to get together, but they also have the potential to create offense, hurt, misunderstanding, and frustration. Being with family is natural, familiar, and often comforting. But both sides of the family can sometimes place unrealistic expectations on newlyweds and put them in awkward, if not impossible, situations. You can also create your own stress by demanding to be with your family of origin during the holidays or demanding to keep all the traditions of your family. Remember that there are two extended families to consider—plus your own new family. Truth is, you can't please everyone all the time, so decide together what's best for the two of you.

You and your future mate should work on your holiday plans before others pressure you into accepting their plans. We suggest that you explore which holidays are important to each of you and why, and then make your plans accordingly. When Dale and I [Susan] were engaged, we talked extensively about this issue. We decided to go anywhere we were invited on Thanksgiving, but we'd stay home on Christmas—and anyone could join us. Once we communicated this to our families, the pressure was off.

Before loved ones get offended by choices you make, communicate your decisions with both families. Sometimes it's best to seek a compromise that seems fair to all families—your new family as well as your families of origin. Does everyone live close enough to combine a celebration? That may be your easiest solution. But more often it's necessary to alternate family gatherings, even if it's not on the exact holiday.

While it's important to respect each other's traditions, you should also create your own unique holiday traditions. What new traditions can you start for holidays like Christmas, New Year's, Easter, or Thanksgiving? Do certain traditions mean more to you than others? Do you want to keep the fruitcake tradition your great-grandmother started? Will Santa be part of your Christmas? Are candied yams a must for Thanksgiving? Are Christmas caroling, trick-or-treating, or Easter baskets important to you?

Dale and I decided to incorporate making my mother-in-law's butter cookies every Christmas, but we also decided to begin a new tradition of having a candlelit dinner at home on New Year's Eve and then enjoying the fireworks shot off Pikes Peak. There are many traditions, large and small, that can help you make your holidays unique, and this in turn will solidify your own family life in special ways.

Later you'll need to consider your children and their needs. You'll also need to consider travel, stress, cost, vacation time, your parents' ages and needs, and so on. Holidays should be enjoyable and restful, so plan ahead when it comes to traveling and visiting family. Spread out your visits wisely, pick your battles, and carefully build healthy relationships.

5. Establish boundaries early on in your family relationships. In order to form your new family well, you must establish good boundaries early on. Always be careful about comparing your families. Try to emphasize the best of each family of origin and honor each in-law family. When one of you criticizes the other's family, it's hard for the other not to feel criticized. If you choose to be critical or harsh with your comments regarding your in-laws, you'll likely hurt your future mate in doing so.

When you marry, you must break the emotional ties of your childhood and make new ties with your mate. To do this, you must develop a new relationship with your parents and family and friends. They all need to understand that things are changing and that your spouse is now your first priority. You must become independent of them, separate from them, and unite with your spouse.

Where you live will affect your relationships with your families. If you live nearby, you'll likely need to set more boundaries than if you live at a distance.

How will you handle visits, get-togethers, and gift giving? What expectations or control issues may need to be discussed in light of your in-laws' personalities? Do you have different spiritual beliefs that will affect your relationships? What if your future in-laws reject your marriage outright? How will you handle that?

First, set boundaries regarding your personal life together as a couple. There should be no secrets between the two of you. Don't share negative information about your mate with your parents or family members, and let your mate know what you do say about him or her to them. It's wise not to discuss the disagreements or struggles you have as a couple with your parents.

Second, fine-tune your physical boundaries. When you're newly married, it can be very frustrating—and invasive—to have family stop by unexpectedly. If you live near your in-laws, ask them to call before coming. Adjust your boundaries as necessary.

Third, establish emotional boundaries. My [Susan's] friend Johanna says that she draws mental boundaries between herself and her in-laws, but she makes sure to always remain respectful. When her in-laws offer advice or "a friendly suggestion," she simply takes it or leaves it. She's forming her new family and knows she doesn't always have to heed her in-laws' advice. Assess every situation—your needs and your in-laws' needs—and if there's a difference of opinion, your relationship with your mate must come first.

Finally, don't assume that your in-laws are going to be just like second parents to you, but do make sure they feel wanted and loved, even if it's not very comfortable. Let them know you care, and respect them as parents.

6. Work through conflicts with your families carefully. In the midst of relating to your in-laws and extended families, there will undoubtedly be times of conflict for you to work through. Remember to "do to others what you would have them do to you" (Matthew 7:12). Show grace and mercy in these situations. A stubborn, inflexible son-in-law or daughter-in-law is hard to live with and is asking for trouble, especially if the in-laws feel that you are making unreasonable demands, are selfish, or have control issues.

Ask the Experts

In *Fixing Family Friction* David and Claudia Arp and John and Margaret Bell write,

> If we're honest, no one has a perfect family—or extended family. Within every extended family exists potential for misunderstanding, hurt feelings, anger, jealousy, fear, and anxiety. But the potential also exists for true communication, mutual understanding, healthy humor, joy, and love.[1]

Fixing Family Friction offers practical and helpful guidance for relating to your relatives. The authors take hundreds of discussions with families who struggle in relationships with relatives and give great ideas for how to relate to your in-laws, parents, and other relatives.

Unresolved in-law conflicts can threaten the joy, intimacy, and peace in your marriage. But you don't have to let that happen! When you have a conflict with your in-laws, if possible talk to your spouse about the hurt feelings or offense before speaking with your in-laws. The two of you may be able to resolve the situation without involving your parents. If it's necessary to confront your in-laws about something, it's important that you be on the same page with your spouse first.

It's also wise not to let misunderstandings escalate into conflicts, but if they do, settle them quickly. Don't let a situation fester, or it could negatively affect your marriage. It might even affect your spouse's attitude toward you, since resentment or hurt feelings can cloud your love and respect for each other. If you and your future in-laws have regular conflicts, we suggest you reread chapter 7 with Ephesians 6:2–3 in mind: "'Honor your father and mother'—which is the first commandment with a promise—'that it may go well with you and that you may enjoy long life on the earth.'"

This mandate isn't just for little children; it's for adult children and in-laws as well. So whenever you encounter a conflict, resolve it in an honorable way. Don't criticize, call each other names, make judgments, or hold grudges. Be positive and respectful, and see what God will do.

Be fair and reasonable when there are problems. If you contributed to the misunderstanding and are wrong, admit your mistakes, apologize, and move on. Compromise when you need to. When hurt happens, recapture joy and peace by forgiving and keeping relationships healthy. When you forgive, you're not only set free, but you also set the other person free.

Extended-family situations can also cause conflict. What about sibling strife or overt favoritism? How will you both handle that? Do either of you have an estranged relative or sibling in your families? One of my [Susan's] friends continually feels caught in the middle between her parents, who have disowned her brother, and her brother, whom she has a special relationship with. Talk about these situations and plan accordingly.

Forming your new family and adjusting to a new way of relating to your families of origin can be challenging. Yet it can also be one of the most rewarding aspects of being married. You once had one family; and now you have three or more. The dynamics of extended family relationships can provide you with a rich history, a wonderful school of learning, and a beautifully full family life—if you let them.

What About Me?

Map out your family tree as far as you can and give it to your fiancé(e). Add one or two words to describe how you experienced each person in your family (successful businessman, alcoholic, funny, grumpy, faithful, manipulative, kind, etc.). Jot down some notes about your family history and discuss these with your future mate.

Ask yourself the following questions and then talk about them with your future spouse:

- Am I too involved with or too disconnected from my parents or family?
- Am I concerned that my future spouse is too close to or too distant from his or her parents or family?
- Am I comfortable with my future in-laws? What concerns do I have?

What About Us?

Discuss your families together:

- What do you like and dislike about your parents? Your family?
- Are there unhealthy patterns, dysfunctions, or other challenges in your family?
- What concerns do you both have about your future in-laws?
- Are you worried about interfering in-laws? What will you do if this happens?
- What are your families' expectations regarding your relationship?

- What are your expectations regarding how your relationships with your families might change?
- Will your families expect to see you regularly? How often?
- What boundaries do you need to set right away?
- What will you do about holidays?
- What family traditions and customs would you like to continue?

Just for Fun!

What moment in your family's history would you like to have witnessed?

Take turns naming two dishes (dessert, breakfast, casserole, etc.) that are special to your family. Consider asking your respective in-laws to share the recipes with you.

What Does God Say?

Here are some important scriptures to consider when relating to in-laws and extended family:

Cursed is the man who dishonors his father or his mother. (Deuteronomy 27:16)

If a man curses his father or mother, his lamp will be snuffed out in pitch darkness. (Proverbs 20:20)

Blessed are the peacemakers, for they will be called sons of God. (Matthew 5:9)

Get rid of all bitterness, rage and anger, brawling and slander, along with every form of malice. Be kind and compassionate to one another, forgiving each other, just as in Christ God forgave you. (Ephesians 4:31–32)

Do nothing out of selfish ambition or vain conceit, but in humility consider others better than yourselves. Each of you should look not only to your own interests, but also to the interests of others. (Philippians 2:3–4)

Whatever is true, whatever is noble, whatever is right, whatever is pure, whatever is lovely, whatever is admirable—if anything is excellent or praiseworthy—think about such things. (Philippians 4:8)

Make every effort to live in peace with all men and to be holy; without holiness no one will see the Lord. See to it that no one misses the grace of God and that no bitter root grows up to cause trouble and defile many. (Hebrews 12:14–15)

12

THE GREAT ADVENTURE

What Do You Do with the Rest of Your Life Together?

Throughout this book you've seen how God views the adventure of marriage. You've learned what a covenant relationship looks like and what the Bible has to say about how we communicate love to each other. Hopefully, you've carefully assessed your personal life and cautiously evaluated your relationship with your future mate. You've also learned tips and techniques on how to deal with needs and expectations, communication and conflict, money, sex, family, and daily living. Now it's time to start the adventure by putting it all into practice.

Consider the journey of the Pilgrims from England to America in the 1600s. They heard God's call to go to a new land. They made plans. They sold most of what they had and made great sacrifices in order to live as Christian families. Then they set out on a great adventure filled with joys and dangers, successes and hardships, and in so doing, they established an incredible future for their children and for future generations.

Marriage is not unlike the Pilgrims' journey. You meet the man or woman you want to marry. You make plans for your future together, and you research and get everything in order to begin the journey. Sometimes you even have to sacrifice things in order to make a life with your future mate. Then you set out together on a lifelong adventure that changes your lives forever.

As on any journey, there are wonderful surprises and times of love and laughter. But there are also dangers, seen and unseen—road bumps, detours, construction, hazards, and difficulties. When you're on a journey, you'll inevitably learn many new things, and you'll grow along the way. You'll enjoy new experiences, meet interesting people, and encounter challenges. And you'll make special memories that will last a lifetime.

Dale and I [Susan] enjoy hiking, traveling, and experiencing new adventures. Whether climbing the Air Force Academy's Stanley Canyon trail in Colorado Springs, literally scrambling up the famous Dunn's River Falls in Jamaica—just as a hurricane hit!—or hiking in the rainforests of Hawaii, we love to experience everything that a journey has to offer. That goes for our marriage as well. We enjoy the good times, make lots of great memories, and capture the moments of fun and adventure. But when times get tough, when hurricanes come or roadblocks hinder our path, we realize that the road bumps and potholes are a part of what makes our adventure unique, so we work together to overcome each obstacle that threatens to impede our journey.

Sometimes your marriage will be easy, but at other times, the potholes or detours of life, the circumstances and the challenges that come your way, will test your marriage and your faith. Yet if you embrace the wisdom of God, He will lead you and guide you through the tough times.

Your marriage is so much bigger than just two people joining forces to journey through life together. If you allow it, your marriage can be a special part of God's bigger story, for you have the privilege of showing others—family, friends, community, and, one day, your children—what God intends for marriage. As you choose daily to intentionally develop your relationship in a godly way, and as you seize the moments to love deeply, treat each other respectfully, and forgive completely, you'll find the journey of marriage to be the most exciting adventure you could ever experience.

START WITH YOUR WEDDING

We honor you for taking the time to read this book and focus on what's really important: your marriage and the rest of your life together. But beware! Too many couples get preoccupied with "the big day"—the wedding. And while the wedding is important, it's only one day, so keeping it in perspective is a wise thing to do.

The wedding industry thrives on making money, and it counts on brides seeing the wedding as an all-consuming grand event. But a Christian wedding should be different. Yes, it should be a lovely experience, a sweet memory, a special time. But it doesn't need to become such a huge production that it overshadows your preparation for your marriage, your future together, or your financial stability. Though it may be a struggle to keep your priorities straight and stay within a budget you and your family can afford, even the simplest wedding can be a memorable and joyous occasion—if you put God at the center of it.

If you really believe God is a crucial part of your relationship, you can use your wedding—the first day of your married life together—to model a God-centered marriage. You can show that you are making this covenant as an active, strategic choice to love your mate through the seasons, changes, challenges, and joys of the marriage journey. As you dedicate your marriage to God during your wedding, you'll reflect and honor Him on this special day and show your families and friends that the promises you're making on your wedding day are sacred ones that will last as long as you both shall live. You'll never regret it.

In preparing for your special day, discuss these questions:

- How can we show our faith in our wedding?

- What do we want to say to each other? To our friends and family? To God?
- What do we want others to remember?
- What is important to our parents? (Be sensitive to them; this is an important day for them too.)

THE WEDDING NIGHT AND THE HONEYMOON

Don't let such an important time as your wedding night get lost in the shuffle of planning your wedding. Be sure you talk about what you expect on your wedding night. Many think it will be "perfect," but be careful not to put too much emphasis on that first night together. Often you're both so tired from the wedding day that you're too exhausted to fully enjoy sex. That's normal. Just enjoy each other, relax, have fun, and recuperate from the events of your wedding. Remember that you'll have your entire married life to grow together sexually.

As with your wedding plans, we suggest you plan your honeymoon within your financial budget so you can focus on your relationship and not worry about going into debt. Although marketers would say otherwise, it's really not important where you go. You may even have to ignore what well-meaning family and friends might expect or pressure you to do. You don't have to go to an exotic island or get so busy sightseeing that you have little time for each other and, as a result, return home exhausted. We also suggest you not plan to go visit relatives or friends. Enjoying your relationship is what's important. It's a big transition to go from being single to being a married couple in less than a day, so take your time and enjoy it.

The busyness of planning for the wedding and reception can be overwhelming, so planning to rest during your honeymoon is a wise thing to do. After all the stress, planning, and celebration of your wedding day, it might be a good idea to even secretly delay your honeymoon departure for a day or two and do something local, then travel when you're rested. It's wise to keep travel arrangements simple and allow enough time for connections. If you're traveling a great distance, be careful not to overdo it, or you might get sick. We chose a cruise because it was so easy and low stress; once we boarded the ship, everything was taken care of—no repacking, meal planning, transportation worries, or anything. This allowed us time to simply enjoy each other.

A good resource for planning your wedding night and preparing for your honeymoon is *The Honeymoon of Your Dreams* by Dr. Walt Larimore and Dr. Susan A. Crockett. Since the honeymoon is often "crucial in setting the tone for your new life as a married couple," you'll find the advice of these doctors timely and helpful.[1]

Ask the Experts

The *Complete Guide to the First Five Years of Marriage* by the counseling staff at Focus on the Family says,

> The sudden change that comes after the honeymoon can be one of life's most sobering moments. Some young couples describe this as "being hit in the face with cold water" or "being struck by lightning." . . . Many couples wonder how the blending of two personalities and sets of ambitions, desires, and dreams could ever be expected by a wise and all-knowing God! Trying to adjust from "freedom" to partnership can be difficult and exasperating—but it's a process, not just a destination.
>
> Here are two principles to remember when moving from independence to interdependence in marriage.
> 1. The feelings are normal.
> 2. It takes work to grow in oneness.[2]

For more practical help on how to successfully blend two lives into one, see the *Complete Guide to the First Five Years of Marriage*.

Take a few minutes and talk through the following questions.

- What are your expectations for your wedding night?
- How have you scheduled rest time for your honeymoon?
- What do you both expect from your honeymoon?

NEW BEGINNINGS

Your honeymoon season should extend far beyond your honeymoon trip. The first few weeks, months, even years of marriage should be a joyous beginning of your lifetime together. It's a foundational time to become one, build a solid team, and grow your roots deep.

Don't expect that everything will be perfect during this first season of your marriage adventure. You may experience fear, awkwardness, disappointment, regret, discomfort, or even conflict. That's not unusual when you're adjusting to any new adventure in your life. Remember those feelings when you got your first job or went to college? It's good to realize that it's only the beginning of your journey, so be patient and allow time for your relationship to grow and mature.

During the first few weeks and months together, it's wise to focus on each other and not get too busy doing things separately. You need time to adjust to living together and time to get to know each other sexually and emotionally. If you keep your schedule free for each other, you'll build a solid foundation for your friendship and intimacy. To avoid getting distracted with things that didn't really matter, we found it helpful to limit most of our media intake as well as extra commitments (sports, social activities, etc.). Instead, we spent all that extra time having fun, talking, dreaming, and loving each other.

You can build a healthy home and marriage right from the start by asking yourselves these questions:

- What should be our priorities as a couple during this adjustment period?

- Are TV shows, the Internet, church activities, sports, or hobbies more important than quality time together?
- Are our friends or jobs more important than building a firm foundation for our marriage?

Don't let these kinds of distractions get in the way of growing a healthy marriage. In today's busy world, you have to take charge and constantly make wise choices. You might also have to break some of the old habits of your single life and make new couple habits. Sometimes this is a bit difficult to do when single friends pull at you or you've been involved in a single-only lifestyle. Yet as you choose to become a team and unite in the plans, purposes, decisions, and responsibilities of your marriage adventure, you'll adjust to the new journey you're on. And remember to occasionally look back at your vision for your marriage and make sure you're working together to meet those goals.

In becoming one, some newlywed couples begin to isolate themselves from others, but that can be a dangerous thing to do. While spending time together is important, try to stay balanced by being connected to a small group and spending some time with family and friends. The truth is that sometimes we need others to help us out. We need community, accountability, and the wisdom of others. We need encouragement and affirmation. If we isolate ourselves, we lose these benefits and more. It's only within the context of community that we can become all God wants us to be.

On the other hand, be careful not to commit to get involved in so much that you neglect your relationship. Decide what's important and helpful to your spiritual and relational growth and get rid of activities and commitments that are counterproductive to building a strong marriage.

As you begin your life together, it's wise to form healthy daily habits of showing affection, giving and receiving affirmation, choosing intimacy, and deepening your life together spiritually. And just doing life together, whether it's running errands, working on a budget, cleaning the house, enjoying family and friends, or taking a walk, can become traditions you establish early in your married life.

Fill this great adventure with love, laughter, work, fun, romance, sacrifice—and forgiveness. And don't overlook the little things that count: be polite, use manners, speak kindly, and always keep dating each other. Most of all, be patient with your future mate and trust God to mature each of you as you become more like Him. He knows the plans He has for you—to prosper your marriage and give you an amazing journey together (Jeremiah 29:11).

Ways to Strengthen Your Marriage

- Be social. Get involved in a Bible study together, and spend time with other couples who will journey with you through life.

- Be friendly. Develop couple friends your age as well as older couple friends who can help you walk out the day-to-day life of marriage.

- Be supported. Find a mentor couple who is a real-life example of a healthy marriage and is willing to help you grow in your relationship with your future mate—a couple with whom you can be honest, open, and accountable.

- Be accountable. Ask a same-gender friend to hold you accountable to holiness in your life.

- Be a lifelong learner. Read books, go to marriage-enrichment conferences and retreats, and keep on learning about your marriage your entire life.

- Be aware. There are seasons in marriage when romance may wane or challenges may feel overwhelming. Never give up on your marriage; work through any trials as a team until you come to a place of mature, unconditional lifelong love. And commit to getting professional help if necessary.

Throughout your marriage, romance will give you the mountaintop experiences you crave, companionship will help you walk through the boring pathways of life, and unconditional love and commitment will take you through the valleys that are less than enjoyable. When you encounter rainstorms or roadblocks, don't ever think of abandoning the journey. Instead, repair the road and weather the storm. When one of you is tired and weary, hold the other up. Encourage each other spiritually and affirm each other in love.

LOVE THROUGH THE YEARS

As the years go by and your marriage deepens and matures, be careful not to get apathetic about your relationship. Remember what a great adventure your marriage has been and can be! As with any journey, there are slow, mundane seasons, but the times of making memories, capturing intimate experiences, and finding quality moments supersede all the rest. Choose not to get discouraged or weary in well-doing, in working at your marriage, in resolving conflict, or in struggling to make ends meet. Build memories that transcend everyday life. It's a daily choice to love and enjoy each other.

It's also good to remember that regular physical intimacy is crucial to a healthy marriage. There will be times you just need to get away as a couple (especially if you have children), so plan to make regular time to do that. We try to take an anniversary trip every year, but others with young children may need a monthly retreat, even if Grandma simply takes the children to her house for the night so the parents get time alone in their home.

When you, your spouse, or others threaten your marriage; when your thoughts, actions, or attitudes draw your heart away from your relationship; when temptations, lies of the media, or the deceitfulness of your own heart tell you it's just too hard; when the lust of the flesh, your own sin nature, or work, things, or mere exhaustion turn you away from your journey together, fight for your marriage. At such times it's critical to regroup, get counseling, and return to the great adventure you've set out to accomplish. Let God lead and guide your marriage and family life, and let Him inspire you, give you new dreams, and help you establish fresh goals.

Marriage is so much about living out your faith on a daily basis. On this great adventure, as you join God in the plans He has for you and your future mate, you can become more like Christ and learn how to reflect Him with your words and actions. You can show the world how God can take two imperfect people and redeem your lives for His glory.

We want to congratulate you as you reach the end of this book! It's our hope that you've learned more about each other, found new ways to communicate and relate to one another, and discovered the tools you need to start your marriage in the right direction.

Thank you for letting us walk this road of preparation with you.

What About Me?

What chapter in this book helped you most? Why?

Name two things you learned about your future mate that you didn't know before.

Are you ready for this adventure called marriage? Why or why not?

Are you ready to weather the storms that may come your way? Why or why not?

Can you commit to allowing the Lord to lead you in your marriage?

Are you now more comfortable and confident you made the right decision to marry?

What About Us?

Are we ready for this adventure called marriage? Why or why not?

Are we ready to weather the storms that may come into our marriage? Why or why not?

Can we commit to allowing the Lord to lead us in our marriage?

Just for Fun!

Take a few moments to talk about your wedding vows. Do you plan to use traditional vows or write your own? What's the significance of making vows to each other?

What would be the best wedding gift you could receive? The worst?

What Does God Say?

Take a final look at God's amazing plan for your lives.

Therefore, I urge you, brothers, in view of God's mercy, to offer your bodies as living sacrifices, holy and pleasing to God—this is your spiritual act of worship. Do not conform any longer to the pattern of this world, but be transformed by the renewing of your mind. Then you will be able to test and approve what God's will is—his good, pleasing and perfect will.

For by the grace given me I say to every one of you: Do not think of yourself more highly than you ought, but rather think of yourself with sober judgment, in accordance with the measure of faith God has given you. Just as each of us has one body with many members, and these members do not all have the same function, so in Christ we who are many form one body, and each member belongs to all the others. We have different gifts, according to the grace given us. . . . Love must be sincere. Hate what is evil; cling to what is good. Be devoted to one another in brotherly love. Honor one another above yourselves. (Romans 12:1–6, 9–10)

"No eye has seen, no ear has heard, no mind has conceived what God has prepared for those who love him"—but God has revealed it to us by his Spirit. (1 Corinthians 2:9–10)

We are God's workmanship, created in Christ Jesus to do good works, which God prepared in advance for us to do. (Ephesians 2:10)

Notes

Chapter 1

1. Al Janssen, *Your Marriage Masterpiece: Discovering God's Amazing Design for Your Life Together* (Colorado Springs: Focus on the Family, 2001), 22.

Chapter 2

1. James C. Dobson and Shirley Dobson, *Night Light: A Devotional for Couples* (Sisters, OR: Multnomah, 2000), 8.

Chapter 3

1. Willard F. Harley Jr., *His Needs, Her Needs: Building an Affair-Proof Marriage* (Grand Rapids: Revell, 2001), 35.

Chapter 4

1. Randy Carlson, *Starved for Affection: Why We Crave It, How to Get It, and Why It's So Important in Marriage* (Carol Stream, IL: Tyndale / Focus on the Family, 2005), 115.

Chapter 5

1. Emerson Eggerichs, *Love and Respect: The Love She Most Desires; the Respect He Desperately Needs* (Brentwood, TN: Integrity / Focus on the Family, 2004), 32–33.

CHAPTER 6

1. Gary Chapman, *The Five Love Languages: How to Express Heartfelt Commitment to Your Mate* (Chicago: Northfield, 1995), 122.
2. 2007 Iowa State University study, cited in Corey Aldritt, "Study: Wives Have Greater Power in Marriage," *Iowa State Daily*, July 6, 2007, www.iowastatedaily.com/home/index.cfm?event=displayArticlePrinter-Friendly&uStory_id=a47557e7-1744-4b03-b3f7-5e04776d0301.
3. Albert Mehrabian, *Silent Messages: Implicit Communication of Emotions and Attitudes* (Belmont, CA: Wadsworth, 1971).

CHAPTER 7

1. Archibald D. Hart and Sharon Hart Morris, *Safe Haven Marriage: Building a Relationship You Want to Come Home To* (Nashville: Thomas Nelson, 2003), 5.

CHAPTER 8

1. Scott Palmer and Bethany Palmer, *Cents and Sensibility: How Couples Can Agree About Money* (Colorado Springs: Life Journey, 2005), 50–51.
2. Federal Reserve Study, 1992.
3. James C. Dobson, *Life on the Edge: A Young Adult's Guide to a Meaningful Future* (Dallas: Word, 1995), 50.

CHAPTER 9

1. Steve Stephens, *Blueprints for a Solid Marriage: Rebuild, Remodel, Repair* (Carol Stream, IL: Tyndale / Focus on the Family, 2004), 6.

CHAPTER 10

1. Clifford L. Penner and Joyce J. Penner, *The Way to Love Your Wife: Creating Greater Love and Passion in the Bedroom* (Carol Stream, IL: Tyndale / Focus on the Family, 2007), 4.

CHAPTER 11

1. David Arp et al., *Fixing Family Friction* (Carol Stream, IL: Tyndale / Focus on the Family, 2008), 8.

CHAPTER 12

1. Walt Larimore and Susan A. Crockett, *The Honeymoon of Your Dreams: A Practical Guide to Planning a Romantic Honeymoon* (Ventura, CA: Regal Books, 2007).
2. Phillip J. Swihart and Wilford Wooten, eds., *Complete Guide to the First Five Years of Marriage: Launching a Lifelong, Successful Relationship* (Carol Stream, IL: Tyndale / Focus on the Family, 2006), 17–18.

Recommended Resources

Arp, David, Claudia Arp, John Bell, and Margaret Bell. *Fixing Family Friction*. Carol Stream, IL: Tyndale / Focus on the Family, 2008. Originally published as *Loving Your Relatives: Even When You Don't See Eye-to-Eye* (Carol Stream, IL: Tyndale, 2003).

Carlson, Randy. *Starved for Affection: Why We Crave It, How to Get It, and Why It's So Important in Marriage*. Carol Stream, IL: Tyndale / Focus on the Family, 2005.

Chapman, Gary. *The Five Love Languages: How to Express Heartfelt Commitment to Your Mate*. Chicago: Northfield, 1995.

Dobson, James C., and Shirley Dobson. *Night Light: A Devotional for Couples*. Sisters, OR: Multnomah, 2000.

Eggerichs, Emerson. *Love and Respect: The Love She Most Desires; the Respect He Desperately Needs*. Brentwood, TN: Integrity / Focus on the Family, 2004.

Harley Jr., Willard F. *His Needs, Her Needs: Building an Affair-Proof Marriage*. Grand Rapids: Revell, 2001.

Hart, Archibald D., and Sharon Hart Morris. *Safe Haven Marriage: Building a Relationship You Want to Come Home To*. Nashville: Thomas Nelson, 2003.

Janssen, Al. *Your Marriage Masterpiece: Discovering God's Amazing Design for Your Life Together*. Carol Stream, IL: Tyndale / Focus on the Family, 2001.

Larimore, Walt, and Susan A. Crockett. *The Honeymoon of Your Dreams: A Practical Guide to Planning a Romantic Honeymoon*. Ventura, CA: Regal Books, 2007.

Palmer, Scott, and Bethany Palmer. *Cents and Sensibility: How Couples Can Agree About Money*. Colorado Springs: Life Journey, 2005.

Penner, Clifford L., and Joyce J. Penner. *The Way to Love Your Wife: Creating Greater Love and Passion in the Bedroom.* Carol Stream, IL: Tyndale / Focus on the Family, 2007.

Stephens, Steve. *Blueprints for a Solid Marriage: Rebuild, Remodel, Repair.* Carol Stream, IL: Tyndale / Focus on the Family, 2004.

Swihart, Phillip J., and Wilford Wooten, eds. *Complete Guide to the First Five Years of Marriage: Launching a Lifelong, Successful Relationship.* Carol Stream, IL: Tyndale / Focus on the Family, 2006.

FOCUS ON THE FAMILY®

Welcome to the Family

Whether you purchased this book, borrowed it, or received it as a gift, thanks for reading it! This is just one of many insightful, biblically based resources that Focus on the Family produces for people in all stages of life.

Focus is a global Christian ministry dedicated to helping families thrive as they celebrate and cultivate God's design for marriage and experience the adventure of parenthood. Our outreach exists to support individuals and families in the joys and challenges they face, and to equip and empower them to be the best they can be.

Through our many media outlets, we offer help and hope, promote moral values and share the life-changing message of Jesus Christ with people around the world.

Focus on the Family MAGAZINES

These faith-building, character-developing publications address the interests, issues, concerns, and challenges faced by every member of your family from preschool through the senior years.

For More INFORMATION

ONLINE:
Log on to
FocusOnTheFamily.com
In Canada, log on to
FocusOnTheFamily.ca

PHONE:
Call toll-free:
800-A-FAMILY
(232-6459)
In Canada, call toll-free:
800-661-9800

THRIVING FAMILY®	FOCUS ON	FOCUS ON	FOCUS ON
Marriage & Parenting	THE FAMILY	THE FAMILY	THE FAMILY
	CLUBHOUSE JR.®	CLUBHOUSE®	CITIZEN®
	Ages 4 to 8	Ages 8 to 12	U.S. news issues

Rev. 3/11

More expert resources
for marriage and parenting . . .

Do you want to be a better parent? Enjoy a stronger marriage? Focus on the Family's collection of inspiring, practical, resources can help your family grow closer and stronger than ever before. Whichever format you might need—video, audio, book or e-book, we have something for you. Visit our online Family Store and discover how we can help your family thrive at **FocusOnTheFamily.com/resources**.

Make the most of your relationships with resources from Focus on the Family®!

From dating and engagement to the wedding and beyond, we're here to help your marriage thrive.

First Comes Love, Then What?

Myths about finding Mr. or Mrs. Right are held to be true by too many men and women searching for that one-in-a-million match. It's time for a reality check. Filled with real-life examples and solid principles, this book will help both men and women learn to use their heads before losing their hearts.
Paperback F00727B

Countdown for Couples

Research and common sense indicate that engaged couples will have stronger, more successful marriages if they participate in pre-marital counseling. Yet with all the planning that goes into a wedding, this important preparation can often be overlooked. *Countdown for Couples* delivers insight in an easy-to-use format and tackles important questions such as: *Are you ready for a lifelong commitment? What should you expect?* And more!
Paperback F00863B

The Savvy Bride's Answer Guide

Your maid of honor might not tell you, but the price of your wedding dress isn't the only thing that may shock you about wedded bliss. During the first year of marriage, you're likely to face all kinds of surprises—from your in-laws' strange traditions to your groom's annoying tendencies. This friendly resource will smooth the road whether you've been engaged for 10 minutes or married for 10 months.
Paperback F00857B

The Smart Groom's Answer Guide

Launching your lifetime love? Getting biblical answers is the smart thing to do! This book provides down-to-earth advice from a team of professional Focus on the Family counselors. You'll get the real story on questions like *What does it mean to be a husband? Why does she want to talk all the time?* And more! Ask now—or forever hold your peace!
Paperback F00856B

marriage

Focus on the Family's Complete Guide to the First Five Years of Marriage

Building and maintaining a good marriage isn't easy, but the rewards are priceless. Focus on the Family counselors present practical, biblical answers to 112 questions commonly asked by recently married spouses. This handy reference empowers couples for a lifetime partnership filled with genuine love and joy.
Hardcover F00271B

Blueprints for a Solid Marriage

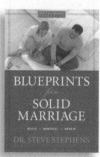

A marriage, like a house, requires time, effort, and regular maintenance. Get immediate practical assistance in this unique do-it-yourself guide to a better marriage. This practical hardcover helps time-strapped couples assess and enhance their relationships with engaging stories and a detailed plan.
Hardcover F00233B

The Language of Love: How to Be Instantly Understood by Those You Love

Words have incredible meaning, especially when they say what you mean. Make the most of your messages by learning *The Language of Love*. It shows how "emotional word pictures" can infuse understanding and intimacy into *all* of your relationships.
Paperback F00227B

Your Marriage Masterpiece

This thoughtful, creative book takes a fresh appraisal of the exquisite design God has for a man and woman. Explaining the reasons why this union is meant to last a lifetime, it also shows how God's relationship with humanity is the model for marriage.
Paperback BL550

The Way to Love Your Wife

With this book, noted sex therapists Clifford and Joyce Penner help husbands keep the passion going and take their marriage to a level that's better than they ever imagined. They cover everything from building desire and enjoying guilt-free sex to getting past sexual problems.
Paperback F00705B